Grace UPON Grace

JOURNALING DEVOTIONAL

Sophie Hudson

B&H
PUBLISHING GROUP

Nashville, Tennessee

Dedication:

To the Briarwood Senior Class of 2022—
I love y'all.

*I am sure of this, that he who started a good
work in you will carry it on to completion until
the day of Christ Jesus.—Philippians 1:6*

978-1-0877-4051-5

Published by B&H Publishing Group
Nashville, Tennessee

Dewey Decimal Classification: 242.63
Subject Heading: GRACE (THEOLOGY) / DEVOTIONAL LITERATURE /
TEENAGERS

Author represented by Alive Literary Agency, www.Aliveliterary.com.

1 2 3 4 5 6 • 25 24 23 22 21

Introduction

*N*ow this may be a slight exaggeration, but I have basically worked with high school students since Moses was a child.

(Just a *slight* exaggeration, mind you.)

I've been a teacher, I've been something called dean of women, and most recently I've been director of student activities at the Christian school where I have worked for twenty-one years. All those years have given me an enormous amount of interaction with high school students, particularly the girls. I haven't always gotten it right, of course—and it certainly hasn't always been smooth sailing. But since students have spent a lot of time in my office, I have asked the Lord to help me be a safe place for them when they needed to talk or vent or maybe just cry while they rifled through my candy bowl and looked for miniature Twix. Whatever gets you through, right?

I'm not a counselor. I'm not an expert. I don't have a lot of initials after my name. (However, if repeated viewings of *Home Town* on HGTV count for anything, then go ahead and hand me my honorary doctorate. I AM MORE THAN QUALIFIED.)

Most of what I know about the struggles and the joys of young women has come from either (1) experience (back in Ye Olden Days I was once a young woman) or (2) listening. I've listened as girls have talked to me during the Stress-A-Thon known as their junior year of high school, or when they've stopped by to visit after their first semester at college, or when we've met for coffee as they're transitioning into grad school or marriage or sometimes even motherhood.

I've said it before, but I'll say it again (ONE MILLION MORE TIMES if necessary): the amount of pressure young women feel these days is enormous. The struggle with perfectionism is huge, not to mention that relational frustrations run deep. And although I can't fix any of that, I love to remind girls what is true:

God's grace is at work here. He is teaching you. He is changing you. He is reminding you how much He loves you. Even when things are hard, He is increasing your compassion and empathy. He is helping you understand something that you need to know.

I believe it with my whole heart. The grace of God—the undeserved love and mercy our heavenly Father lavishes on His children—changes everything. Covers our sin completely. Draws us closer to the heart of Jesus. Reminds us what matters most. Teaches us what we would never learn on our own.

And that's just the tip of the grace iceberg, my friends.

So for the next 100 days, we're going to talk about that grace. And some other stuff too. I pray you'll be encouraged in your faith, comforted by God's love, and challenged in your relationship with the Lord.

I don't know what led you to pick up this book, but I am so honored you're here. It is my absolute joy to share these words with you. And finally, please feel free to dig through the imaginary candy bowl until you find your favorite. (I will warn you that the Twix are, as always, in short supply.)

Love,

Sophie

Day 1

I have to tell y'all: observing the life of our seventeen-year-old son is kind of fascinating. I talk to so many girls every day who are stressed or worried about different parts of their lives, but if I had to give one word to describe Alex's general mood, it would be *unbothered*. He is rarely stressed. Breezy, even. I'll point out an upcoming test or project, and he'll shake his head, smile, and say, "No worries, Soph!" (He calls me "Soph," by the way.) "I'll get it handled!"

For reasons I cannot explain, Alex Hudson lives in a place of unshakable confidence and optimism. He loves playing football, but then last year he totally surprised his daddy and me by announcing he was trying out for the spring musical review (he did the same thing again this year). He gets a huge kick out of people, he laughs a ton, and his favorite food group is wings. Sure, he can be a jerk about the dumbest things, but mostly he is wide open to whatever a day holds. I love him a lot, if you can't tell.

Recently I overheard Alex and a friend talking about their favorite Mexican restaurant, and the friend said that the restaurant's salsa is sometimes too spicy for her. Alex piped up right away to disagree, and after a little bit of back-and-forth about the merits of the salsa, Alex said, "Hey, if it's not spicy, I'm not interested!" They laughed and moved on to a different (though equally riveting, I'm sure) topic, but I'll have you know that I thought about Alex's comment for the rest of the day.

Not just in terms of salsa, you understand.

So often, we want life to be mostly exciting and adventurous (and yes, maybe even a tiny bit spicy). We push back against what seems ordinary or maybe even boring, and if we find ourselves in the same routine day after day, week after week, we wonder if we've gotten something wrong or missed some thrilling opportunity along the way.

I think that's why Alex's comment about the salsa got my attention. Because "spicy" is great and all, but a nonstop diet of it isn't necessarily sustainable (I'm talking in terms of living, but that's probably also true in terms of eating). Plus, when we're forever focused on life being some endless, rip-roaring ride, we can miss the grace of simple, beautiful joys: a sunset, a baby's laugh, a lazy day with a friend, a Sunday afternoon nap, or a leisurely hike with the family. We're not made to live on full blast from sunup to sundown; we need time to rest and read and play and create. We need time to think and pray and ponder. We need to recharge.

Can life be an absolute blast? It certainly can. Can it be mind-numbingly boring? You'd better believe it. Is every bit of it grace? One hundred percent. By all means, enjoy the spicy, but don't forget to live fully in the mundane. The Lord does some of His very best work in the most ordinary places.

Live and love your real life today.

READ 1 TIMOTHY 6:6–8.

1. Are you more drawn to big adventures or to regular life? Do you like a balance? Or do you maybe believe that regular life *is* a big adventure?

2. What's the most adventurous thing you've ever done?

3. What are some ordinary things in your life that make you really grateful?

4. Take a couple of minutes to be completely quiet. Write down what you notice.

_____

_____

_____

_____

TODAY'S PRAYER

_____

_____

_____

_____

_____

_____

_____

_____

_____

_____

_____

_____

_____

_____

_____

Day 2

$\mathcal{I}$ don't know where you're sitting right now, but I'm currently sitting in my little office at our house, thanks to the first day of a very unexpected break from school. For the last twenty-one years I have worked at a local high school, currently as our director of student activities (this essentially means I am the school's cruise director), and yesterday our superintendent announced we will be out of school for an indefinite length of time because of the pandemic that currently has all the world on its heels.

It's the middle of March. It's springtime. It's the beginning of the fourth nine weeks (that means something to those of you who are currently in school). It's supposed to be the season for baseball and soccer and track and junior/senior prom. It's supposed to be the point in the year where teachers start to wrap up their courses, AP exams loom maybe a little too near on the horizon, and seniors plan graduation celebrations. It's supposed to look so much different from this.

But here we are. And I'm gonna make a bold statement: *it's weird.* We're not even three weeks into this temporary new normal, and I feel like my perspective has changed in the craziest ways: a deli offering curbside delivery is a beautiful sight to behold, a forty-five-minute walk at the park is downright life-giving, and don't even get me started about my profound gratitude regarding the two big packs of toilet paper we still have in our storage room.

A lot of times, I think, we want to jump past the weird to the moral of the story. We want to get to the part where we have a handy two-sentence summary of *Hey, here's what that was all about.* Assigning some meaning can feel easier than sitting in the tension of what we don't understand, especially when we're frustrated that things aren't turning out like we hoped.

Given all of that, I am trying to remember that this, too, is grace. There is grace in the weird, in the unknown, in the unexpected. Because when confusion threatens to steal our peace, we can remember and cling to what is true:

1. The Lord loves us with an everlasting love (Jeremiah 31:2–4).

2. The Lord is our comforter (2 Corinthians 1:3–4).

3. The Lord works all things together for good (Romans 8:28–30).

When you're in a time or season that feels uncertain, you can look to these truths day after day, knowing that even when life is weird, Jesus holds all things together. This morning, in fact, I read some comforting words from Paul David Tripp: "The hardest things in your life become the sweetest tools of grace in his wise and loving hands."[2]

Rest in His grace today.

READ JEREMIAH 31:1–6.

1. What feels uncertain or even shaky to you right now?

2. As you read today's Scripture passage in Jeremiah, what comforted you?

1. Paul David Tripp, *New Morning Mercies: A Daily Gospel Devotional* (Wheaton, IL: Crossway, 2014), March 31.

3. Can you think of something difficult in your life that ultimately drew you closer to God?

_____

_____

_____

_____

4. What three things feel like God's grace in your life right now?

_____

_____

_____

_____

TODAY'S PRAYER

_____

_____

_____

_____

_____

_____

_____

_____

_____

Day 3

As long as I can remember, I have loved watching television. I'm well aware that my love of TV might not be the most, um, *academic* part of my personality. But for what it's worth, I don't watch just to numb out and disconnect from my real life. I watch because one of my favorite things in the world is getting absolutely immersed in a story.

Recently one show absolutely captivated me. It's a docuseries about four doctors who work in a New York hospital, and two of the doctors are neurosurgeons. They perform multiple brain surgeries a week, so it's obviously a high-pressure, high-risk situation every single time they scrub in for a procedure.

Given the demanding nature of their work, I sort of expected that the neurosurgeons on the show would move through their days by disconnecting, by depersonalizing the sometimes very grim situations their patients face. I was oh-so-wrong, however. The doctors actually begin each procedure by sharing the story of the person on the operating table. They share the person's name, family background, work, medical history— sometimes even anecdotes about interactions with that particular patient. These are world-class surgeons, but their care for their patients is *personal*. They are committed to the care of a person whose story they have taken the time to know, and they want every other person in the operating room to know that story as well.

I don't know if you've thought about it lately (and no shame if you haven't, because clearly I needed a TV docuseries to remind me), but these doctors are a reminder of how Jesus cares for us. He knows it all, my friends. He knows our strengths, He knows our weaknesses, He knows our sin, and He knows our shame. He knows where we hurt, who we love, and how our future turns out. There's a reason we don't have to introduce ourselves to Him every time we pray: He knows who we are. And not only that: our stories are safe in His care.

I keep thinking about the deep, assuring grace of being known. As Jesus sees us, loves us, and directs us, He does every bit of that from a place of complete knowing. You don't have to earn His interest; you don't have to demand His attention. Just like the surgeons in the TV show are very closely attending to the needs of their patients, Jesus (and I think it's safe to say that Jesus is, you know, on a whole 'nother level) is very closely attending to the needs of His children. In every situation, He is your fiercest advocate. And every single day of your life, He is your safest place for help and health and healing.

Walk into today with the assurance that you are completely seen, completely known, and completely loved. What grace. What a Savior.

READ 1 CORINTHIANS 13:8–13.

1. Write out verse 12 from today's reading.

2. When you consider the fact that you are "FULLY known" (emphasis mine), how does that make you feel? Explain with a few words or phrases.

3. Is it easy for you to let people really know you? Or do you tend to keep pieces and parts of you tucked away?

_____

_____

_____

4. Is there an area of your life that needs some extra attention or care from the Lord? A place where you need some spiritual or relational surgery, so to speak? Talk about that a little bit.

_____

_____

_____

_____

TODAY'S PRAYER

_____

_____

_____

_____

_____

_____

_____

_____

_____

_____

_____

Day 4

*O*ne of my favorite things in life (that's a big statement; I'll stand by it) is to go walking at a park by our house. I'll probably mention my walks at least seventeen more times in this book, mainly because the Lord seems to teach me a lot when I'm outside. This is possibly because my walks are one of the few times in the day when I'm actually, you know, *quiet*, but we certainly don't have to get into that right now.

I'm grinning.

A month or so ago I had just reached the top of the first big hill on my favorite part of the trail when I noticed the very strong scent of pine. Initially I couldn't figure out where it was coming from, but just around the curve I spotted a giant pine tree that must have been chopped down the day before. The trunk of the tree had been sawed into fifteen or twenty pieces, and that part of the trail basically smelled like a Christmas tree farm. The scent of pine was so fresh that it was almost invigorating, and as I walked past the newly felled tree, I marveled at the fact that something that had been so beautiful to look at could also smell so amazing.

In the days that followed, however, I realized that the scent of that gorgeous pine tree was becoming more and more faint. The longer it was disconnected from its life source—its roots and the soil that surrounded them—the less distinctive its scent. One day I even walked right up to the logs, leaned over, and sniffed as hard as I could. The pine aroma was discernible, but barely; the fallen tree mostly just smelled like the rest of the park.

The same thing happens with us. When we're staying closely connected to the Lord through Scripture, prayer, and the power of the Holy Spirit, we carry His presence—His fragrance—everywhere we go. But when we allow ourselves to move away from the Source of our strength, our purpose, and our hope, we start to lose our distinctiveness. Our spiritual aroma, as it were, starts to fade, and over time it blends in with the world around us.

The good news, however, is that, as people who believe in God and agree with Him that Jesus is the atonement for our sins, we don't have to suffer the same fate as that big ole pine tree. If we feel we've drifted away from our ultimate Source of life—if we have somehow tried to convince ourselves that staying connected to Him isn't necessary—we can reconnect. Remember: the Lord is kind, and He is gracious. He wants us to be fully established and rooted and growing in Him. So when we admit to Him that we've been stubborn or shortsighted or prideful—when we get honest about desiring the abundant life that only comes from and through Him—He mercifully lets us superglue our roots right back on to the strong, living tree. Soon we're smelling like pine (that is to say: Jesus!) again.

And by His grace, He won't just keep us alive in Him; He will enable us to thrive in the places where He plants us.

What a wonderful gift from a wonderful God.

READ 2 CORINTHIANS 2:14–17.

1. Have there been times in your life when you have felt disconnected from God? What was that like?

_____

_____

_____

_____

_____

2. When (or where) do you feel the most connected to God?

_____

_____

_____

_____

3. Are there specific areas of your life where you have a tendency to think you're self-sufficient? Like you can manage it on your own? Explain.

_____

_____

_____

_____

4. What are some daily practices that encourage and strengthen you in your connection with God?

_____

_____

_____

_____

TODAY'S PRAYER

_____

_____

_____

_____

_____

_____

_____

_____

Day 5

*F*or the bulk of my adult life I would have described myself as a Certified People Pleaser. I'm not saying I won any trophies or anything, but I could have for sure qualified for some certificates of achievement or maybe even some blue ribbons. I was really good at it.

About six or seven years ago, though, the temptation to keep everybody happy started to lose its grip on me. There are a bunch of reasons why—maybe meet me at Starbucks later, and I can share a few—but the biggest was that I started to realize I was being bossed around by what the Bible calls "fear of man." I didn't want anyone to be unhappy with me, so I would say whatever I needed to say to keep the (fake) peace. And one of the problems with living that way was that in all my efforts to keep people happy, I wasn't always telling the truth.

One passage in Scripture has been enormously encouraging to me as I have tried to shake loose of my people-pleasing tendencies. In Luke 1, Elizabeth and her husband Zechariah were at their son's circumcision with friends and family. Scripture tells us that the neighbors and relatives wanted to name the child Zechariah, after his father, but Elizabeth stood firm: "No. He will be called John." After Elizabeth wouldn't give in (and please keep in mind these people loved our buddies E and Z; they weren't their enemies), they questioned her answer by petitioning Zechariah. Zechariah, who was mute at the time, also stood firm by writing his answer: "His name is John."

Here's the thing: Elizabeth's pregnancy was miraculous. In fact, her pregnancy was prophesied by the angel Gabriel in what was the first utterance from God in more than four hundred years. The reason Zechariah couldn't speak at the circumcision was he had questioned the prophecy and had promptly been made mute. So more than nine months later, with their new baby right in front of them, Elizabeth and Zechariah knew their child was a fulfillment of God's promise. And since Gabriel had also told Zechariah that the child's name would be John (Luke 1:13), there was no

15

way "Zechariah Jr." was a viable option. Elizabeth and Zechariah were going to be obedient to what God said. "His name is John."

Right after Elizabeth and Zechariah stood their ground, three things happened: (1) Zechariah could speak again, (2) he began praising God, and (3) people talked about baby John all throughout the hill country of Judea. Elizabeth and Zechariah didn't try to explain, they didn't go out of their way to make sure everyone understood their decision, and their obedience ultimately gave credibility to John's calling (Luke 1:66).

What a reminder that when the Lord gives us clear instruction, our job is to stand in that spot. We don't have to overexplain, we don't have to make sure everybody is okay with what we're doing, and we don't have to work for our certification in people pleasing. Because when we know how the Lord has called us and directed us, we get to stand there. Confidently.

And fear of man has nothing on that.

READ LUKE 1:57–66.

1. Can you think of a time when someone tried to change your mind about something? What was the issue, and how did you respond?

2. What's the difference between standing your ground because of conviction and standing your ground because of pride?

3. What is something you feel compelled to stand up for in the here and now?

_____

_____

_____

_____

4. Proverbs 29:25 says, "The fear of mankind is a snare, but the one who trusts in the LORD is protected." What does that mean to you?

_____

_____

_____

_____

TODAY'S PRAYER

_____

_____

_____

_____

_____

_____

_____

_____

_____

_____

_____

_____

Day 6

*O*ur house was built in 1974, which means she is officially middle-aged. Over the last few years, my husband, David, and I have pulled in some professionals to update the house a bit. We've replaced our kitchen counters, added a new backsplash, painted the exterior, and spruced up the garage. The house may be in her late forties at this point, but she is KICKIN' IT right now.

One of the biggest changes was in our living room, specifically its dark, tealish green walls. I didn't mind the green for the first few years we lived here, but it had started to feel outdated. So we hired the world's greatest painter, Nicholas (to be honest, I don't know of an official painter competition, but we believe with our whole hearts that Nicholas and his team would win), and he covered the dark teal with a creamy beige called Manchester Tan. When I tell you the new color absolutely transformed our living-room life, I am not exaggerating. It brought so much light and airiness into the main part of the house, and we delighted in the transformation for about five weeks.

Until one morning when David saw a big leak in our bathroom ceiling.

He quickly called in a pro again, and we were relieved to hear that the bathroom ceiling would be an easy fix. But what concerned the repairman much more was a big, nasty leak coming from our shower. I have no idea how David and I had never noticed it. Since the leak was inside the wall, we had to call a restoration specialist to determine how much it had damaged the tile in the shower and the floor joists in our basement.

A few days later, David and I met with the kindest restoration specialist. He said ultimately the best option for the long-term health of the shower was to rip it out and rebuild. Since we wanted to address any residual damage and not just put a Band-Aid on the problem, we agreed. About a week later, the restoration specialist's crew tore our bathroom down to the studs. There was water damage, mildew, and even a little bit of mold. It was a bigger job than we expected, but after careful cleaning and rebuilding, the bathroom now functions better than it ever has.

So often, I think, we want the makeover. We want things to look prettier and shinier and newer. That's what happened when we painted our living room. And it was great! But sometimes, we need more than lipstick; we need full-blown restoration. And, oh my goodness, it is pure grace to be able to get to the all-the-way bottom of a problem, to dig deep and tear out whatever is rotten and not working anymore.

Remember today that your Restoration Specialist is at work. Through Scripture, through the Holy Spirit, and through His people, He is moving us in the direction of repentance and restoration. By His grace, He is changing us in the ways we need most.

Trust Him in the process. He is making all things new.

READ 1 PETER 5:6–11.

1. Is there an area of your life where a makeover has seemed preferable to restoration? (I'll go first: I have really struggled with anger the last few years.)

2. Why do you think we can be resistant to getting to the bottom of a persistent problem?

3. On a scale of 0–5 (0 being "not at all" and 5 being "completely"), where are you in terms of trusting God to help you as you deal with your problems? Think about your answer and then explain. (There is no shame in your honesty. He can handle it!)

_____

_____

_____

4. Look at verse 10 of today's reading. What are the four things "the God of all grace" will do for you?

_____

_____

_____

TODAY'S PRAYER

_____

_____

_____

_____

_____

_____

_____

_____

_____

_____

Day 7

$\int$ was having breakfast with a friend when a topic we had never discussed somehow made its way into our conversation. Yes, it was one of those topics people say should never be discussed at the table—there's lots of potential for a difference of opinion to turn into an argument, I guess—but since my friend and I have known each other for a really long time, it seemed like a fine thing to talk about. So we did.

To my surprise, my friend and I didn't just disagree a little bit. We deeply disagreed. We still do, in fact. And after so many years of friendship, I remember feeling some degree of shock to realize we were on opposite sides of the issue. We eventually agreed to disagree and moved on with our conversation as well as the meal, but I couldn't help but wonder if the long-term dynamics of our friendship would shift as a result.

It's been several years since that breakfast, and here's what I know: my friend has continued to love me, and I have continued to love her. Has the topic come up again? Yes. Did we eventually come to agreement on that particular topic? No. Has the world come to a fiery end as a result of our disagreement? Nope. Believe it or not, Earth is still spinning on its axis and everything.

No doubt, thousands of issues can worm their way into our friendships and threaten to disrupt our preferred levels of peace and harmony. Some of those issues are more inflammatory than others (in the case of my friend and me, it was a political one). Unexpectedly, though, that ongoing area of disagreement with a friend I love so dearly has taught me a few things:

1. We want to make sure we love our people more than we love our opinions (another friend actually said this to me a couple of years ago). The last thing I want is for my relationships to be bossed around by whatever has me fired up during a news cycle. So people first. Always.

2. It may seem easier to love people when our beliefs and opinions align. But in my experience, when we ask the Lord to help us set

our opinions aside and love people like He would—without any bias or judgment—He comes through over and over again.

3. I never would have believed this when I was younger (because I'm a 9 on the Enneagram and peace is THE BUSINESS for me), but it's actually really good that we don't all agree on everything. If we constantly interact with a bunch of people who are essentially our mirror images, we have no need for Jesus' grace and mercy, which enables us to love and prefer others in ways we simply cannot do in our own strength. He changes all of us for the better by teaching us how to bear with one another in love.

Sometimes we forget, but in all situations, He is able. Even when we disagree. How about that?

READ EPHESIANS 4:1–6.

1. What are one or two issues you're passionate about?

_____

_____

_____

2. How do you respond when you find yourself in disagreement with friends or family members about those issues?

_____

_____

_____

_____

3. Write out Galatians 5:22–23.

_____

_____

_____

4. Do you see those qualities in yourself when you're in disagreement with someone? Circle two or three you feel compelled to pray about.

_____

_____

_____

_____

TODAY'S PRAYER

_____

_____

_____

_____

_____

_____

_____

_____

_____

_____

Day 8

*F*or as long as I can remember, I have loved to cook. Even after being married for roughly seventy-two years (give or take), I still enjoy getting in the kitchen late in the afternoon and figuring out what to make our family for supper. It doesn't hurt that my husband and son are very grateful eaters, but still. The process of chopping/mixing/stirring/sautéing/roasting continues to be something I really enjoy.

What I do not enjoy nearly as much is baking. Oh, I'll make the occasional cake, but mostly I don't like the precision and repetition that baking requires. I don't want to make four dozen of anything, I don't want to deal with delicate layers, and I have zero interest in icing techniques. I would rather make six batches of cornbread dressing than one batch of cookies. I recognize my aversion to baking is a little weird, but I'm okay with it. I hope we can still be friends.

Even though I personally don't love to bake, I very much enjoy watching TV shows where other people bake. My favorite is a baking show from England (it's delightful). The contestants' challenges are so demanding that I would no doubt weep openly and curl up beside my baking station if I had to do even a third of what is required in each episode. But since these contestants are insanely talented and—clearly— super enthusiastic about the baking arts, it's great fun to watch.

One of my favorite parts of watching this particular show is seeing how contestants respond to adversity—and seeing how vastly different their reactions are from what might be typical in America. For example, let's say a contestant's soufflé falls. In America we might be tempted to blame the oven or to prove how capable we typically are—maybe even going so far as to list all the other soufflés we've made that turned out perfectly—but our British friends accept their failures with a much different attitude. "Oh, it is quite dreadful," one competitor might say. Another might shake her head, apologize, and size up her soufflé by saying, "It's certainly not the most attractive dish, now is it?"

I have to tell you: it's a level of humility I find disarming and even endearing because the contestants' humble responses indicate that they are teachable. They want to get better. They don't want to blame anyone else for what went wrong; they want to learn the lesson and move forward.

Over the last few years, I have reminded myself that in the face of disappointment or adversity, I want to respond like the bakers do. I want to own my mistakes without being defensive or blaming other people. I want to be humble, and I want to be teachable. Can you even imagine what we might learn from the Lord if, in the wake of our own mess-ups, we resisted the urge to point fingers? If we took responsibility for whatever we have (or have not) done without trying to shift the blame to someone else?

If the bakers can teach us some lessons, just imagine what Jesus can do.

READ PSALM 25:4–7.

1. What's your typical reaction when you mess up? Do you get angry? Super hard on yourself? Ashamed? Write about that a little bit.

2. What is a recent mistake you've made? How did you handle it?

3. Why do you think it's so easy for us to point fingers at other people and blame them for our mistakes?

_____

_____

_____

_____

4. Look at verse 7 in today's Scripture reading. What adjective describes the Lord's love? What does that mean to you?

_____

_____

_____

_____

TODAY'S PRAYER

_____

_____

_____

_____

_____

_____

_____

_____

_____

_____

_____

Day 9

If you drive through my part of the city, you will likely see a lot of geese. Yes, you read that correctly. Literal gaggles of geese gather in this part of town, and although the geese haven't actually told me why they find our zip code so appealing, my best guess is it's the abundance of small lakes and ponds. If water is a goose attractor, then our neck of the Birmingham woods is most definitely a magnet.

The geese pretty much run the show at different points in the year—they block traffic, they monopolize trails at the park, and during gosling season, the geese parents will hiss like snakes at anyone who gets too close to their babies. These geese, although beautiful, can be a bit of a hazard in the day-to-day.

A month or so ago I had just gotten out of my car at the grocery store when I spotted about ten geese across the parking lot. I quickly realized it was two separate gaggles, and they seemed to be racing toward a good-sized water puddle just a few feet away from me. It had rained most of the morning, so the puddle held plenty of water for all the geese to enjoy, but one of the gaggles had no intention of sharing. As I stood next to my car, fascinated, I watched the goose who first arrived at the puddle do his level best to intimidate the other gaggle—hissing, charging, and flapping his wings.

After twenty or thirty seconds of trying to fend off his attacks, the second group of geese gave up and walked off. I could hardly blame them. That puddle was convenient, but it certainly wasn't the only watering hole in town.

I thought about those geese for the next couple of hours. Something about their behavior felt uncomfortably familiar. That first gaggle was unnecessarily territorial—unnecessarily hostile, even—especially because the other geese just wanted a drink of water. As best I could tell (and granted, my knowledge of goose-related relational dynamics is limited), that first goose perceived a threat where there was absolutely no threat. SIMMER DOWN, everyone.

And the more I pondered "The Tale of the Geese and the Publix Puddle," the more I realized how much their behavior reminded me of what I've seen in other people and what I've seen in myself. We're better than geese at disguising it, of course, because we're human, but in general we can be pretty good at perceiving threats where there are none. We also have some skill at being unnecessarily territorial, whether that's with group texts or inside jokes or even cafeteria tables. We will excuse this behavior in ourselves, but that doesn't make it right. What we know deep down, of course, is when we walk and live with Jesus, we get to live with open hearts and open hands—willingly, joyfully welcoming and sharing.

So. Here's a lesson courtesy of some Birmingham geese: life with Jesus ensures plenty of room for others and plenty of grace to share. We have no need to guard the metaphorical water puddles. (I'm assuming it goes without saying that we shouldn't hiss or flap our wings.) Walk into your day with wide open arms.

READ ROMANS 15:1–7.

1. Can you think of a time when you have acted a little bit like the territorial geese? When you have been on the defensive because you perceived a threat or maybe you just didn't want to share?

2. What are some places in your life where you're most likely to be unnecessarily territorial? With family? Friends? Something you love to do?

3. Have you ever felt unwelcome? Has that experience changed how you treat (or welcome) others? Talk a little bit about that.

4. When we give in to a territorial mentality, what is the lie—or lies—we're believing?

TODAY'S PRAYER

Day 10

*F*or about six years I served as dean of women at the school where I work. The best way to describe that job is that I was sort of an on-campus mama—someone to help with the day-to-day challenges of high school—and this basically meant that my primary responsibilities were listening, handing out Kleenex, and providing an obscene amount of chocolate. It also meant that I had a front-row seat as girls would talk about their faith and where they were in their relationships with Jesus.

It has been a few decades since I was a high school student trying to integrate my faith into my life, but I can still tell you what my three biggest defaults were during those initial days, weeks, and years of figuring out what it meant to follow Jesus:

1. Trying to be the "good girl" who looked like she had life with Jesus completely figured out, or . . .

2. Setting myself up as the unofficial monitor for how everybody else was managing their relationship with Jesus, but mostly . . .

3. Feeling discouraged and frustrated because both #1 and #2 were deeply unfulfilling and also not at all the end goal of a life marked by faith in Jesus Christ.

I struggled on a lot of levels, and honestly, my struggles weren't short-lived. Eventually Colossians 3 put some things into perspective for me. Verse 3 reminds us that our life is hidden with Christ, and verse 4 tells us that Christ is our life. In both cases the original Greek for *life* is *zoe*—pronounced ZO-A—and according to *Strong's Lexicon*, the meaning of *zoe* is this: "The absolute fullness of life, both essential and ethical."

As believers, we can get so caught up in trying to live a "perfect" Christian life that we forget we have been given fullness of life in the only One who is actually perfect. And we can be encouraged by another of *Strong's* definitions for *zoe*: "life real and genuine, a life active and vigorous, devoted to God." For so long I thought the proof of my faith was in my behavior; I didn't understand that my focus should always and only be the Lord. This is so liberating! We can stop chasing a man-made illusion of perfection, because what we really want is a *zoe* life. We want to stay tethered to the Lord, absolutely—we don't want to stray far away from our life source—but we can stay attached to Him and still have some room to move. We can pursue the things that light us up from the inside out. We can glorify Him everywhere we go.

Where we get into trouble—and where we fail to cooperate with God's work in and through us—is when we try to create fullness of life in our own strength. Maybe we find ourselves doing things for the approval of people and not God. Or maybe we're so preoccupied with our reputation as a "good Christian" that we don't struggle in the open. Maybe we're stingy with grace and often hold other people to an unreasonable standard. The bottom line is that we can check off a lot of religious boxes and never know the freedom of "life real and genuine . . . devoted to God."

Consider today if you're living like you know where life is. And if you feel like you've been working so hard at creating a Christian life for yourself that you've almost forgotten that He is your life, remember the assurance of Psalm 23:1 (NCV): "The LORD is my shepherd; I have everything I need."

READ COLOSSIANS 3:1–4.

1. Why do you think it can be such a temptation to monitor other people's spiritual lives instead of tending to our own?

2. Read Colossians 3:2 out loud. What are some of the "earthly things" that distract you in your life with the Lord?

_____

_____

_____

3. What do you think it means to live a *zoe* life?

_____

_____

_____

4. What is something you really love to do? How can you devote that particular thing to God? Could it maybe even be a form of ministry to others?

_____

_____

_____

TODAY'S PRAYER

_____

_____

_____

_____

_____

_____

_____

Day 11

I typically love to travel, but a few years ago, on a trip to Texas, I found myself more than a little homesick. I was there to speak at a church, but my school was playing in the 5A football state championship back home in Alabama, and I had a massive case of FOMO. Still, I trusted I was where the Lord wanted me, and I resolved to push through.

So. That evening, when I arrived at the church where I was speaking, I was looking forward to a great night. However, when I was getting out of the rental car, I saw a warning on the dashboard: "Key Battery Low." I had a lot on my mind, so I didn't think too much about the key or its battery issues, and I headed into the church.

Three hours later, I left the church, happy to have spent time with some wonderful women and a little bit sad because my school had lost the state championship game in a close contest. I ran through a drive-through so I could grab a quick (late!) supper, and by the time I pulled into the hotel parking lot, three things were abundantly clear: (1) I was tired, (2) I was hungry, and (3) I really, really needed to go to the restroom. I was just about to hop out of the car and book it to my hotel room when three little words stopped me in my tracks: "Key Battery Low."

Needless to say, this reminder was deeply inconvenient, especially since my need for a restroom was a solid 9.8 on a 10-point scale. There was some urgency, my friends. And after I realized that my key fob wouldn't lock my doors or open my trunk, there was a different kind of urgency about how I planned to crank the rental early the next morning to get to the airport. For several minutes I did my best to figure out what to do next—repeatedly trying the key fob—all the while trying to mind-over-matter it in an effort to stave off my very, um, *insistent* bladder. Finally I determined I was going to have to call the rental company, and as I eased my way out of my seat and to the back of the car where my phone was, my bladder decided it was no longer interested in my drawn-out negotiations. I could hardly process what was happening, but I stood right there in the Marriott Courtyard parking lot and wet my pants like a champion.

It was a low, to say the least. And by the time I made it to the room, showered, contacted the rental company, fixed the key fob problem, and washed my pants in the hotel room sink (true story), I fell into bed tired and discouraged. I was in a strange-to-me city, I had missed my school's game, and I had lost all control of my bladder in a hotel parking lot. Not to mention that I had to leave for the airport in less than six hours.

But when I landed in Birmingham the next morning, I discovered that snow had blanketed my beloved city. As I (slowly!) drove home, I couldn't get over how beautiful everything looked—and how the previous night's events paled in comparison. Every turn brought a new, awe-inspiring view, and I was reminded that sometimes, when life doesn't go like we hope, or we miss being with people we love, or we soak our pants like a toddler's romper (hey, it happens), the Lord surprises us with the grace of something beautiful, the grace of fresh perspective, the grace of pausing to take in His creation.

And on a day when you expect it the least but just might need it the most, that beauty . . . well, it will be enough.

READ PSALM 104:10–26.

1. When was the last time you felt out of sorts—whether you were homesick, discouraged, or maybe even embarrassed?

2. How did you respond? Did you let yourself feel your feelings, or did you try to push through? Or maybe even just laugh it off?

3. Have you ever found yourself in awe of God's creation? Explain.

_____

_____

_____

_____

4. How does God comfort us and encourage us through His creation?

_____

_____

_____

_____

TODAY'S PRAYER

_____

_____

_____

_____

_____

_____

_____

_____

_____

_____

_____

Day 12

I'll just go ahead and admit it: sometimes I snore a little. Oh, I like to think that I lie down at night and fall asleep on my back and breathe evenly throughout the night like a delicate princess, but the truth is that on nights when I'm particularly restless (too much caffeine, anyone?) (too much anxiety, anyone?), my sleep can be fitful and maybe even disruptive to my husband. Because I'm snoring.

On the rare occasions (and I'm just sticking with the phrase "rare occasions" because it makes me feel better about myself) when my snoring wakes up my husband, he will generally tap me on the shoulder and say, "Roll over, please." Doing something as simple as turning my head the other direction will typically stop my snoring pattern, and then I sleep better and he sleeps better and everybody is happier. But true confession: sometimes I don't want to roll over. Sometimes I want to stay in the same spot in the bed because it's comfortable or it's warm or I just don't really have a mind to move. So sometimes my stubborn, sleeping self tries to pretend I don't hear David's voice. Sometimes I don't want to do what he asks. Sometimes I just want to stay right where I am.

The spiritual parallel here is like a big flashing red light, isn't it? Because my goodness, is there ever a difference between stubbornness and convictions. It's generally right and good to stand on our convictions because those are the places Jesus would have stood. So we don't have to give in when it comes to our beliefs about who God is, about the authority of Scripture, about the power of the Holy Spirit. We don't have to compromise on the big stuff, even if we feel like someone is trying to convince us to move or shift from what we know is right.

However, sometimes we dig in on smaller issues because of pure, old-fashioned stubbornness. Sometimes we pretend to be standing on really important Christian convictions when we're really just being stubborn to protect our own rightness or comfort level. We have to be willing to examine that. It's the same with the challenges of the day-to-day: we refuse to reschedule a meeting or a study session because we think the other person should have managed their calendar better. We refuse to apologize for our part in a misunderstanding with a friend because we decide she was more in the wrong than we were. We refuse to consider someone else's opinion about a current event because it's not the same as ours. We refuse to listen to a teacher's wise counsel because it's not what we want to hear.

The bottom line is that our persistent stubbornness can get us in a mess. When we combine stubbornness with our perceived rightness, we're in some straight-up prideful territory. And as I have learned over and over again in my life—because make no mistake, I have been covered up in my own stupid stubbornness and pride at times—Proverbs 16:18 is no joke, my friends: "Pride comes before destruction, and an arrogant spirit before a fall."

Today is a great day to evaluate if you're sitting in stubbornness and calling it conviction. The good news is that we serve a God who is merciful, who forgives us when we confess our sin. What a gift to be able to stand in His grace. We need it every single day.

READ PHILIPPIANS 2:1–5.

1. What are two or three issues or situations where you know you're being super stubborn right now? Or where you've been stubborn recently?

2. What would it look like for you to let go of the stubbornness? What might happen?

3. Can you think of a time when pride caused you to (figuratively) stumble or fall? Explain that a little bit.

4. What are two or three issues or situations where you know you're operating out of conviction (in other words, you're standing in a place where Jesus would stand)?

TODAY'S PRAYER

Day 13

*N*ot too long ago I started a thirty-day Bible reading plan of the Gospels (Matthew, Mark, Luke, and John). My first day's reading assignment was Matthew 1:1–17, where Matthew breaks down the genealogy of Jesus, starting with Abraham and then working through a forty-two-generation patriarchal hall of fame including Amminadab, Rehoboam, and Zerubbabel, among others. Fortunately, I've listened to an Andrew Peterson song called "Matthew's Begats" enough times that I have a pretty good idea how to pronounce everyone's names. But the familiarity didn't stop a fresh realization: even though I've read this passage before, I got to the end and thought *Well, it feels like it took a long time to get to Jesus.*

Don't we all feel that way sometimes? Like, in one way or another, it's taking us a long time to get to Jesus? Like maybe we're going through something difficult and wondering when we'll get to the part where Jesus comes back and makes everything better?

I thought about this the day I read Matthew 1, and I'm still thinking about it now. In fact, as I write this day's devotional, our country is in the middle of a pandemic, and everything has been upside down for months. My husband has been working from home, I've stopped going to my job at school, we're wearing masks everywhere we go, and if the pandemic weren't enough, I learned for the first time in my whole life that there is an insect called a murder hornet. This year has been no joke, and in moments of deep heartache and sadness over a virus we still haven't been able to stop—as well as a fresh reckoning with continued racial injustice in this country—I have found myself imagining how Jesus would tend to the sick and the hurting and the heartbroken. I've pictured how He would comfort people who feel afraid. I have longed for Him to make all things new.

And here's what I have to remind myself in the middle of all the hard stuff: Jesus is already here. The King is here. He is with us. Here's what that means:

1. **Jesus is our friend** (1 John 2:1-2). He sees us. He hears us. He talks to our heavenly Father on our behalf. He loves us.

2. **Jesus teaches us and corrects us in Scripture** (see the Gospels). When we read the words He spoke, when we see how He treated people, when we witness His compassion, when we remember His sacrifice for us on the cross—we have an instruction manual for what it looks like to represent His heart for people in our broken world.

3. **We get to carry the presence of Jesus wherever we go** (1 John 4:17). Right now may not be the appointed time for Jesus to return to earth to rule and reign. But Jesus in us—His Spirit in us— can bring peace, grace, mercy, and love in the middle of sadness, confusion, frustration, and change.

What encouragement to remember we're not just on a journey *to* Jesus. We're on a journey *with* Jesus. Thanks be to God.

READ JOHN 14:25–27.

1. Do you more often feel like you're on a journey *to* Jesus or a journey *with* Jesus? Maybe a little bit of both? Why is that?

_____

_____

_____

2. Has anything in your life lately made you long for Jesus? Explain that a little bit.

_____

_____

_____

3. Based on what you know of Jesus, how do you think He might respond to the situation you mentioned in question 2?

4. Who are some people you know who love others like you imagine Jesus does? What specific traits do you see and admire in them?

TODAY'S PRAYER

Day 14

About eight years ago we had to replace the roof of our house. This is not exactly something a homeowner looks forward to with excitement and anticipation, but it's just one of the necessary responsibilities of keeping a house in good working order. A stable roof keeps out wind, sun, and rain; so from that perspective, a functioning roof feels like a solid housing strategy.

After the new roof was installed, my husband and I were inordinately proud of it. It was pretty (as much as asphalt shingles can be pretty), it looked sturdy, and it made us feel like we had done something super responsible for the long-term health of the house since the roof was supposed to last for thirty years.

You probably have a hunch where this is going. For a while, the roof looked great. But about three years ago, we noticed that some places looked like they were beginning to sag, sometimes even like they were holding water. We dealt with a leak here, a leak there, and with the roof's warranty long since expired, we tried to convince ourselves that the roof would stop deteriorating and do its job.

About a month ago we asked our favorite repairman to take a look at the integrity of the roof, and he confirmed what we suspected: it wasn't installed properly. The roofer had used the wrong size boards and the wrong clips, so over time, the boards warped, and they can no longer adequately support the shingles on top of them. The best way to explain it is *we have ourselves a mess*, and we're going to have to replace it much sooner than we expected. So, you know, that's a real bummer.

As I've thought about the roof (and I've thought about it a lot—insert angry emoji here), it has reminded me of all the ways I have knowingly or unknowingly constructed some (figuratively) bad roofs in my life. Maybe I used the wrong material to fix something, or maybe I skipped a critical first step in an important process, or maybe I settled for something that looked fine on the outside but structurally couldn't go the distance. I've done this in all sorts of ways: in friendships, in taking care of my health, and in my relationship with the Lord, just to name a few.

Fortunately, it's never too late to learn from our mistakes. About twenty years ago, for example, I realized that my views of the Lord were often dependent on my emotions because the foundation of my faith had some pretty big gaps. The Lord kindly began some serious repair work. I put myself under the instruction of wise, thoughtful Bible teachers, and over time, sound (and loving!) teaching from Scripture filled those foundational gaps. By God's grace, I came to a greater understanding of who God is, who I am in Him, and how specifically He directs us when we seek His guidance through prayer and reading His Word. We will always have to endure some storms, but His covering—His roof—is loving and sure.

Hopefully we'll eventually be able to say the same about the roof of our house. But no matter what happens with those boards and shingles, I am forever, deeply grateful for the patient repair work of our heavenly Father. Amen.

READ MATTHEW 7:24–27.

1. Are there any areas of your life where you feel like you're in need of some repair work? In this case we're talking internal, not external. Elaborate on that a little bit.

2. Do you think your relationship with the Lord has ever been more focused on how you're feeling than it is on what you know to be true about Him? Why does that matter?

3. Have you ever been tempted to settle for a quick fix in a relationship or in a situation at school or work? Why is the quick fix oftentimes so appealing?

_____

_____

_____

4. Look at Matthew 7:24 again. At this stage of your life, what does it mean to build your house "on the rock"?

_____

_____

_____

TODAY'S PRAYER

_____

_____

_____

_____

_____

_____

_____

_____

_____

_____

Day 15

*O*ne of my very favorite things about working at a high school has to be the sports. I flat-out love all the parts of all the sports. I love sitting in the bleachers, I love cheering for the players, I love watching a tight competition, and I love celebrating a big win. I am not kidding one bit when I tell you that my affection for a live sporting event is so strong that I would happily attend a tiddlywinks competition, and even though I don't necessarily know what all that would entail, I feel pretty safe in saying that I would paint up for it. As you do.

Several years ago, our boys' soccer team was playing for the 5A state championship, and whether you're a sports fan or not, you no doubt know that playing for a state championship is a big deal. We had lost in the semifinals the year before, so we had some high hopes. A huge crowd of supporters traveled to the game two hours away, and everyone, while optimistic, poised themselves for a tough game.

I don't know that our team was surprised at all—they were confident and determined going into the game—but our fans were surprised (and delighted!) when we quickly built up a 4-0 lead. There was always the possibility our opponent would mount a comeback and snatch a come-from-behind victory, but as the game went on, our fans became increasingly optimistic that "state champions" would forever be a term associated with that year's soccer team.

Sure enough, our guys won in a 5-0 shutout. As the final seconds ticked off the clock, the revelry began, and when time finally expired, our players ran jubilantly across the field, chest-bumping and high-fiving and shouting with everything they had. I've watched the video of their celebration eight or nine times, and the best way I can describe it is that they were like a jumping blob. Their collective joy transformed them into a moving mass of euphoria, and it was, in a word, *fantastic.*

After about twenty seconds of full-on hysteria, one of our players broke off from the pack and began to run across the field. He stopped when he reached one of the opposing team's players who was bent over, sobbing, and clearly devastated by the loss. Our player leaned down and put his hand on the other guy's shoulder. I have no idea what he actually said, but it was obvious that he was speaking words of encouragement, showing great compassion, and empathizing with the other player's heartache. To this day, I'm convinced that even in light of the 5A State Championship trophy our players brought home, the way our player noticed and responded to someone else's hurt was the real win.

No doubt the Lord gives us opportunities for well-deserved celebration, and man, is it ever fun to savor those times. But even in the middle of that, let's not miss how He also gives us opportunities to really see one another, to respond, and to set aside our own interests for the sake of someone else's comfort. Be on the lookout for how you can extend God's care today. For the person who is hurting—and even for people who may be watching— those moments can be game changers.

READ LUKE 6:43–45.

1. Can you think of a time when someone has lovingly responded to you when you were hurting? What did that mean to you?

2. Who are two or three people in your life who do a great job of loving other people? How does seeing that kind of care in action encourage you?

3. Do you know someone who is hurting right now, whether from short-term or long-term disappointment or pain? How can you pray for that person today?

4. What are some ways you could encourage that person (in addition to praying, which is awesome)?

TODAY'S PRAYER

Day 16

*W*ithout question, my husband, my son, and I all share an obsession with our dog, Hazel. We all delight in spoiling her rotten (true story: for breakfast, she likes her eggs scrambled, *thank you very much*) and making sure she lives at an optimal level of comfort at all times. As a matter of fact, she is curled up next to me as I type this, lying on her very favorite blanket. Also, she is snoring.

Life with Hazel is not always so peaceful, however. Hazel was separated from her mama and littermates when she was a puppy, and she came to live with us not too long after that. So she is inordinately attached to us and deals with a crazy amount of separation anxiety. She is happiest when we're all at home, and if one of us makes a move to, you know, *put on socks*, she starts to pace and bark like she can convince us that putting on shoes and leaving the house is the dumbest idea ever. She calms down after we're gone, but the anticipation of one of us leaving is almost more than her doggy heart can bear.

Over the years, Hazel, who is the epitome of all bark and no bite, has developed some interesting ways of "protecting" us. When we take her outside for a walk, if she thinks there's a chance a delivery truck or a baby-strolling neighbor might be at the top of the driveway—because maybe she thought she heard something forty-five minutes or seven hours ago—she will bolt out our front door and bark like crazy at her imagined foe. She can't charge up the hill, of course, because she's on a leash, but even the barking is totally unnecessary since *Hey, Hazel, you're directing all manner of fear and angst at the mailbox. That's all that's there.*

We do this, too, you know. Oh, we might not be quite as obvious about it as Hazel is, but when we're operating from a place of fear or insecurity, we can perceive threats when what we're actually facing is something akin to a mailbox—and our "mailboxes" can take lots of forms. Maybe a broken friendship has made us hesitant to trust, so we assume that other people don't have our best interests at heart. Maybe relational abandonment by someone we love has convinced us that we need to protect ourselves at all costs. Maybe continued unkindness from an authority figure has persuaded us to strike first with our words so that people don't get a chance to hurt us.

As believers, though, we don't have to live on the defensive like sweet Hazel does. That's because we can operate from a place of peace, confidence, and belonging. The Lord is our protector and our shield. We don't have to keep our eyes peeled for imagined threats, nor do we have to stay crouched and tense, ready to charge at whatever we fear might be disruptive to our personal peace. We can relax. Trust. Know that our identity and security depend not one iota on anything on this earth. Because in every moment of every day, the care and compassion of our Father in heaven holds us, carries us, and sustains us. As children of our gracious, merciful, loving God, we have absolutely nothing to fear. Praise His name.

READ PSALM 8:1–9.

1. Are there any ways you think you might be a little like Hazel? Any areas where fear tends to boss you around? Explain.

_____

_____

_____

_____

2. What is the current "mailbox" in your life? What's the thing you're tempted to view as a threat even though it's actually harmless?

_____

_____

_____

3. What situations tend to put you on the defensive? When do you feel yourself (figuratively) crouching down and ready to bark?

_____

_____

_____

4. Reread Psalm 8:4. How does the Lord look after you?

_____

_____

_____

TODAY'S PRAYER

_____

_____

_____

_____

_____

_____

_____

_____

_____

_____

_____

Day 17

I love to make a playlist. Maybe something about the whole process is a little ingrained in me because I grew up creating many a mixtape with my dual-cassette boom box (please, try not to be too impressed). Regardless of the reason, I am usually working on a new playlist at any given point in time, and lately, my playlist building has become such a big part of my days that I wouldn't be one bit surprised if someone calls me from Apple Music and says, "MA'AM, THANK YOU FOR YOUR PATRONAGE BUT MAYBE YOU JUST NEED TO LEAVE ALL THE SONGS ALONE."

One playlist I've listened to the most is called "Great Big Praise." It's an assortment of gospel music that has brought me great comfort (and also inspired some great big praise, as it were) during my daily walks around the park. It's full of big voices and big declarations, and the song I've had on repeat more than any other is called "Holy Water." It's a song by a group called We the Kingdom, and the version that's been my companion features Tasha Cobbs Leonard, an incredibly gifted singer who I pray will be my vocal instructor in heaven. #PleaseTasha #ThankYouInAdvance

The lyrics from "Holy Water" are gorgeous, but the part that moves me the most isn't anything in the verses or the chorus. There's a section in the middle of the song where the vocalists improvise and pray out loud while the instruments play softly in the background, and around the five-minute mark, my good friend Tasha (I don't actually know her) (CALL ME, TASHA) sings a line that's not part of the formal lyrics: "Something about your grace"—and then, after a short pause—"makes me want to change." A few measures later, she echoes her improvisation: "Oh, I want to change."

Every time I listen to that part of the song, tears fill my eyes. That declaration—"I want to change"—is such a huge piece of growing in our faith, isn't it? It isn't easy to admit the areas where we struggle, to confess what we're not getting right, to examine our hearts and our minds under the guidance of Scripture and the Holy Spirit. What grace that we can humble ourselves and not feel defeated; what grace that we might be compelled to ask the Lord to help us change.

And then there's this: when we see how the Lord really does have the power to change us—when we remember that, in His mercy, He shows us a new way forward in the middle of our cries for His help—we can't help but worship Him. We can't help but give Him the honor and praise and glory He deserves. It would be enough that He loves us just as we are when we come to faith in Him. But He doesn't leave us there. So when He convicts us of an area where change will make us more like Him, it is a gift of grace to agree with Him and to ask Him to help. He is so trustworthy. Praise Him today for His faithfulness and His loving direction. We can be thankful that we get to change and grow as He leads.

READ PHILIPPIANS 3:12–16.

1. Watch or listen to the version of "Holy Water" I mentioned above. Write down a few sentences about how the Lord ministered to you through what you saw/heard.

_____

_____

_____

_____

2. As a general rule, is change easy or hard for you? Do you like it, or do you resist it?

_____

_____

_____

_____

3. Is there an area of your life where you can honestly say "I want to change"? If yes, what is it? And if no, can you remember a time when you knew that change was necessary for you to grow deeper in your relationship with Jesus?

_____

_____

_____

_____

4. What are some qualities you aspire to in your life with the Lord? Consistency? Humility? Obedience? Teachability? There are all kinds of answers, so just jot down the first three or four that come to mind.

_____

_____

_____

_____

TODAY'S PRAYER

_____

_____

_____

_____

_____

_____

_____

_____

_____

_____

Day 18

*I*n Luke 8:22–25, Jesus told His disciples to join Him in a boat to go to the other side of a lake. The disciples hopped in, as most people would be quick to do when receiving a travel request from Jesus, and they began their journey. As they made their way across the lake, Jesus fell asleep, and that was probably all well and good with the disciples until they found themselves in the middle of a storm. With wind whipping and the boat filling with water, they totally panicked and woke Jesus up. Scripture tells us they said, "We're going to die!" (v. 24).

How did Jesus respond? He stilled the storm. And He and the disciples made it to the other side of the lake. So initially these four verses in Luke 8 might seem like an "all's well that ends well" situation, but we can take away several reminders as we live and walk with Jesus here on dry land:

1. The disciples are on a boat with Jesus. They know who He is. They have seen Him at work. And still they are a hot mess in the middle of the storm. We do the same thing. We walk with Him and communicate with Him. I think all of us would say that we trust Him. But we, too, can be a hot mess in the middle of whatever storm we're navigating, whether it's spiritual, relational, familial, educational—we could go on and on.

2. The second part of this verse is comforting because it reminds us of Jesus' power: "He got up and rebuked the wind and the raging waves. So they ceased, and there was a calm" (v. 24). And just like that, in the aftermath of panic, there was peace. So often a deeply felt need will convince us we need to take charge, spring into action, come up with a plan, control everything in sight, manage all the details. But here peace came on the scene because of what Jesus did, not what the disciples did. We want to be wise, of course; but ultimately our peace comes from a Source we cannot manufacture in our own power.

3. At times we have likely responded a lot like the disciples (that is to say: white hot panic). In the middle of the unexpected, even as people who live and walk with Jesus, we can still forget how He can intervene and transform a seemingly impossible situation. The end of this passage makes me smile because we see Jesus and the disciples exchange questions: "Where is your faith?" Jesus asked, and in response, the disciples said, "Who then is this? He commands even the winds and the waves, and they obey him!" (v. 25). He reminds them what they need, and they remember who He is. The same is true of us.

Finally, there's this: I know not one of us is Jesus. But as we live and lead and love in our regular, everyday lives, let's be sure, through the power of the Holy Spirit, to extend the comfort and care that Jesus has shown us. Let's be mindful of how we can help calm (figurative) storms, take care of people, and bring order to chaos and peace to confusion.

He will get us to the other side.

READ LUKE 8:22–25.

1. Can you identify any current storms in your life? Any areas where you feel like the waves are threatening to overtake you?

2. Write out a sentence or two and tell the Lord about the situations where you're anxious or maybe even a little panicked.

3. Why do you think the disciples said, "We're going to die!" in verse 24 instead of just saying "Can You help us?" What does their reaction tell us about how we often respond in a crisis?

_____

_____

_____

_____

4. Who are some friends or family members who are enduring storms right now? How could you pray for them?

_____

_____

_____

_____

TODAY'S PRAYER

_____

_____

_____

_____

_____

_____

_____

_____

_____

Day 19

My walks at the park are my therapy. During tough seasons, I go there almost every day to exercise and clear my head, so you can imagine my disappointment last year when I realized that I had pulled a calf muscle. You can also imagine my disappointment when I realized that a calf muscle injury can be really painful.

Because I've never really been an athlete—just a mom who likes to walk—I don't always know how to navigate the line between *Ow, that hurts a little bit* and *Ma'am, you are officially and indefinitely sidelined.* So with the pulled calf muscle, I kept pushing, convinced that I could keep going and eventually "work it out." Well, one morning I was trying to power through the pain, walking a little more slowly than usual, when I ran into a friend who was also walking. After we had talked a few minutes, we decided to keep walking together. Sounds like a great plan, right?

Well, normally it would have been. But on that particular day, I was struggling to accommodate the pain in my calf, and my friend, out of habit, was walking at her normal speed, which is somewhere between "fast" and "potential world-record pace." By the time we had made it a half mile, my calf muscle was practically screaming, "SLOW DOWN, YOU DUMMY," but my pride was telling me to keep going. I easily could have said, "Hey, I'm gonna have to hang back a little," but instead I continued to pretend I wasn't in an enormous amount of pain.

Eventually my calf won the battle, and I told my friend I was going to have to stop. She could not have been more compassionate and understanding. But I've thought about that day a lot since then because it's a reminder of how tempting it can be to pretend like everything is okay when it actually isn't. It's a reminder of how pride can keep us in a situation that's unwise or even painful. And I'm not talking about walking anymore, if you haven't picked up on that.

Here's the thing: when you're dealing with something painful—whether it's the result of injury or heartbreak or illness or maybe even sin—it takes courage to be brave enough to say, "Hey, I'm hurting, and I can't keep up right now." What I failed to remember that day in the park is the grace of a compassionate response from a friend. Because whether it's your calf or your head or your heart that's causing the pain, pride screams that we just have to suck it up and keep going. Grace, however, sings a different refrain. Grace says, "It's okay—we can slow down together" or "How about we just sit right here for a while?"

Being able to honestly communicate how we hurt and how we're struggling—without fear of judgment or shame—is one of the great gifts of grace in Christian community. We may be prone to forget (and the pull of pride can be powerful), but with grace, you get to be honest about how you're really doing. You get to slow down. You don't have to pretend like everything is okay (and, in my case, end up having to ice and elevate your stupid leg for the next week). The Lord and His people will meet you right where you are.

READ JAMES 5:13–16.

1. Can you think of a time when you've tried to pretend like everything was okay even though it wasn't? Anything like that going on now?

_____

_____

_____

2. Why is it so hard to be honest with people when we're struggling, no matter what kind of struggle it is?

_____

_____

_____

_____

3. On some level do you feel like you need to slow down right now? In what area? Explain that a little bit.

4. Look up the song "Great Is the Lord" by Jonathan McReynolds. As you listen, write down lyrics that encourage you.

TODAY'S PRAYER

Day 20

*O*n most days it takes me nine minutes to drive to work. It's such a short commute that it isn't even an option to listen to talk radio or a podcast; there's just not enough time to jump into a news story or a narrative. So I usually listen to about two and a half songs—maybe a voice message from a friend—and before I know it, I'm pulling into my parking spot. Easy breezy.

If there's a hiccup in the process, it happens when I have to turn out of a subdivision and onto the road where my school is. There's no stoplight at the intersection—just a stop sign—and there is rarely a lull in the traffic. That means I am almost always dependent on the kindness of others to turn onto the main road. I've wondered many days if I could petition for a stoplight, but in fourteen years of driving that route to work, I have never gotten stuck at that intersection, and I've never had to turn around. Someone always lets me make that tricky left turn. Someone always helps me out.

The same thing is true in life, of course. From time to time we'll find ourselves in places where it feels like there's no way out, and we'll be stuck there forever. Maybe it's the heartache after a break-up, maybe it's watching a family member endure something difficult, or maybe it's a particular area of sin we just can't seem to shake. No matter the reason, those hard spots are precisely where we find ourselves grateful for people who are willing to lean in and love like Jesus. Their help likely won't be as simple as making room for someone to turn onto a busy road, but the grace of their attention and care will hopefully make a way for us to turn toward healing and hope.

We will all need help at some point—and we will no doubt be humbled and relieved to receive it—but as believers we also need to recognize when it's our turn to offer help to others. In these moments we'll find ourselves on the other side of the intersection, so to speak, and we'll get to experience the grace of extending a helping hand. This won't be because we're so selfless and awesome and on the lookout for chances to play superhero;

it will be because Christ is at work in us, teaching us how to look after our loved ones and our neighbors (ones we know and ones we don't) even when it's inconvenient. It will be because through our own hardships, the Lord has been building empathy and compassion in us. Even in the most mundane situations—picking up an elderly person's mail, running errands for a neighbor whose parent passed away, dropping off a smoothie for a sick friend—our empathy and compassion are reflecting our Father's heart. That's why our hope is always that people see Him and not us.

Sometimes we need help. Sometimes we're the helper. What a gift to both give and receive the grace of a helping hand. What grace to love one another in the middle of the big and small challenges that come our way each day.

READ 1 JOHN 4:7–12.

1. Is there a particular challenge you face almost every single day? Explain that, and keep in mind that it might not be something practical like traffic; it might also be an emotional or a spiritual challenge.

2. Are you dependent on others as you deal with that challenge? How so?

3. Is it typically more comfortable for you to give help or receive help? Why do you think that is?

4. Look up 2 Corinthians 1:4. Why does God comfort us in "all our affliction"?

TODAY'S PRAYER

Day 21

$\mathcal{N}$ot too long ago I joined some dear friends in Nashville for a ministry event. I drove up the afternoon before the next day's event so that I could settle in my hotel room, finish editing a podcast episode, and hopefully not feel as rushed. And listen, my night was delightful. The hotel was quiet, my editing time was productive, and I even managed to catch up on email. Look at the Lord!

The next morning I woke up early so I would have plenty of time to let my face wake up before rehearsal (listen—this is a whole thing after you hit your forties . . . although your body may wake up, your face is all *I believe I still need a minute*). By the time I walked out of my hotel room, my face was awake, I was relaxed, and I couldn't wait to see some people I love a lot.

When I unlocked my car, I noticed that it didn't make the same sound it normally does, but I didn't think much about it. But when I opened my door and the alarm went off, I wondered what in the world was going on. It felt like it took five minutes for my brain to make sense of it all—in reality it was a few seconds—but as I mashed buttons on my key fob to try to get the alarm to stop, I noticed that the inside of my car was in total disarray. My passenger window was shattered, glass was everywhere, and the contents of my glove compartment littered the seats. Even stranger was the damage to the inside of the car; my backseat console was broken in half, my dashboard was gouged and scratched, and someone had clearly tried to pry my interior light panel from the ceiling. On top of that, there were streaks of blood everywhere, it seemed.

It was a fine how-do-you-do for sure. But thanks to some great friends, a kind policeman, and a nearby glass company, the immediate aftermath of the break-in wasn't as disruptive as I had feared. When I got home, though, the real challenges began. After visits to two body shops, who-knows-how-many phone calls with our insurance company, and three times the cost we expected, my car was finally, completely fixed—three months after the break-in.

The whole process was a reminder of how difficult it can be to fully restore something, whether that's a busted-up car interior or, more likely, a relationship with another person or a relationship with God. Here's the thing: sometimes we're affected by damage we had no part in creating. Sometimes we find ourselves all up in the middle of brokenness we didn't choose—something like a parents' divorce, a family illness, or prejudiced treatment by others. And more often than not, it feels like it's taking a sweet forever to make things right. So remember: grace is at work in these places. That doesn't mean it's fun, and that doesn't mean it's convenient, and that doesn't mean it will all happen according to our personal timetables, but the Lord will give us what we need at each point in the process.

Trust the Lord with wherever you're in need of restoration today. He is making all things new.

READ REVELATION 21:1–5.

1. Have you ever witnessed someone you care about walking through a process of restoration? Were there ways you extended grace in that process?

_____

_____

_____

_____

2. Is there an area of your own life where there's an almost nagging need for restoration? Explain.

_____

_____

_____

_____

3. What are some of the emotions you experience when restoration—or fully fixing something that is broken—feels slow?

4. When you think about the passage in Revelation that you read today, what encourages you?

TODAY'S PRAYER

Day 22

As I write this I'm beginning my twenty-first year at the high school where I work. It's hard for me to believe I've been there so long, especially since I was twelve my first year on the job.

Oh, I kid. But this next part is dead serious: when you work with high school students a long time—particularly the girls—you see more than your fair share of friendship drama. In fact, I have witnessed so much friendship drama that I am well over my required lifetime quotient, which means NO MORE DRAMA FOR ME. I have fulfilled my obligations. Nothing but peace and harmony from now on, thank you for your cooperation.

Truth be told, though, the dynamics of friendship have fascinated me since I was in high school. On one hand, the Lord has been so gracious to give us the joy of knowing one another and enjoying deep relationships. But what I have seen over and over again is how fear will jump in the middle of the relational equation and throw everything off balance. That fear might look like insecurity or jealousy or pettiness or possessiveness, and it will jack up a friendship in record time.

It takes discernment to know if your friendship has been hijacked by your unreasonable expectations or the other person's negligence (or vice versa). It's all too easy to cast blame when we're hurt by or disappointed in a person we've considered a friend, so we have to do some honest relational reflection. Are you constantly bending over backward to keep someone happy? Do you feel like you have to sacrifice pieces and parts of your faith to keep the peace with someone? Do you tend to be controlling? Do you find yourself wondering how to keep the other person on lockdown, monitoring his or her every move? Because if that's the case, it's time to examine that. After all, this is a friendship; this is not code yellow.

Scripture reminds us often that deep, lasting relationship is built on a foundation of love. True, God-centered friendship prefers someone else's interests over our own, not because we're trying to keep the other person happy, but because we want to "love as he first loved us" (1 John 4:19). We have the privilege and the responsibility to love one another well, so we need to consider how well our friendships reflect the love of Jesus. If you find that fear or uncertainty in those relationships is a recurring theme, ask the Lord for wisdom about how to handle that. Talk to an older friend you trust. No relationship is perfect, but if you feel constantly off-kilter, it's good to consider why. The Lord can handle the drama, but He isn't the source of it.

For believers, healthy friendships are an extension of our relationship with Jesus, and those friendships don't require us to alter our personalities or opinions to keep someone else happy. The joy that comes from loving one another, caring for one another, and ultimately getting the biggest kick out of one another's company flows freely from the security of understanding how lavishly Jesus loves us. What a friend we have in Him.

READ COLOSSIANS 3:12–14.

1. In general, do you feel like your friendships are healthy and life-giving? Do you feel like they energize you? Why or why not?

_____

_____

_____

2. Have you ever been in a friendship that felt unhealthy? Or where you felt like you had to compromise your faith? How did that relationship affect you?

_____

_____

_____

3. Look up the lyrics to the hymn "What a Friend We Have in Jesus." Write out the verse that resonates with you the most.

_____

_____

_____

_____

4. Are there any friendships where you need the Lord's help to be healthier/less possessive/less controlling? Explain.

_____

_____

_____

_____

TODAY'S PRAYER

_____

_____

_____

_____

_____

_____

_____

_____

_____

Day 23

*O*ver the last ten or so years, I have become a Certified Sunset Chaser (because that's totally a real thing, right?). There are few things I enjoy more than when God paints the sky with pinks and oranges and blues. And if I happen to be at the park or beach or some other scenic place, then all the better. I'm always awed by how a sunset reveals God's creativity, and I always feel closer to Him when I get to stand (or sit) in the shadow of His setting sky. For me a good sunset never gets old.

A few months ago, my friend Stephanie texted to let me know that the sunset was especially beautiful at her house, so I hopped in my car and tried to figure out where I might get the best view. I could just see a sliver of it over the tops of the trees, and since we live in a fairly hilly area, I knew I needed to get to the highest point possible in the quickest amount of time. Within a few minutes I was parked at a nearby fast-food restaurant, car windows down, happy as could be that I had managed to catch a glimpse of the final, brightly colored brushstrokes of another summer night's masterpiece.

As I drove home, I couldn't help but giggle at my appearance. I was wearing pajama bottoms and flip-flops and sporting day-three post-workout hair that looked like it might require CPR, but none of that stopped me from being beyond grateful for the beauty I had just witnessed.

And here's what I kept thinking about.

For a sunset to be truly magnificent, there has to be some cloud cover. A day with nothing but clear blue skies is gorgeous for sure, but the sunset that follows a cloudless day may not look all that remarkable. However, when clouds are present to filter the light—well, that's when God really shows off. As the setting sun cuts through the clouds, the light is shocking, the light is transforming, and the light—with all its beautiful colors and angles—is pure grace.

Sure, we tend to think we prefer living "cloud-less" lives. We don't want anything to interfere with the sunshine. But sunsets remind us that God does some of His most stunning work as He overlays the clouds and the sun, using the light to pierce the darkness and transforming the ordinary into something awe-inspiring and extraordinary.

And what we know is that He doesn't just do this with the sky. Maybe one reason I love sunsets so much is because they make me think about all the ways I've seen the Lord make something beautiful out of the mundane, the gray, and the not-so-pretty—in my life, in my family's life, in my friends' lives. Transformation is His specialty, and seeing it in action never gets old.

Behold our creative, merciful, gracious God. Today—even right this very second—He is making something beautiful.

READ PSALM 104:31–35.

1. What is something in nature that makes you extra aware of God? Snow? A rainy day? The ocean? A beautiful sunrise?

_____

_____

_____

_____

_____

2. How do you feel when you witness this particular thing? Comforted? Awed? Something else? Explain.

_____

_____

_____

_____

_____

_____

3. When was the last time something beautiful stopped you in your tracks? How did you respond?

4. How are the beautiful parts of creation God's grace to us?

TODAY'S PRAYER

Day 24

One of the realities of walking with the Lord for a long time—or even just hearing the gospel for a long time—is that we can grow numb to it. The good news of Jesus starts to feel more like regular ole news, and while we don't forget that Jesus took on our sin as His own to save us from the consequences of our sin, it's almost like we lose our active remembrance of the wonder of salvation. We lose sight of who we are apart from the saving grace of Jesus.

In the book of 2 Peter, our good friend Peter (we don't actually know him) (he was a little hot-headed, but I feel like we would all win him over) gives us some clear instruction about how to avoid growing numb in and even dismissive about our faith. Starting in chapter 1, he writes, "Make every effort to supplement your faith with goodness, goodness with knowledge, knowledge with self-control, self-control with endurance, endurance with godliness, godliness with brotherly affection, and brotherly affection with love" (vv. 5–7). It's not just that we're supposed to keep *going* in our walk with the Lord; we need to keep *growing* as well. We need to constantly put what we believe into practice because, as Peter writes in verse 9, "the person who lacks these things is blind and shortsighted and has forgotten the cleansing from his past sins." So we want to be people who *remember*.

How do we do that? How do we fight apathy and feeling disconnected from our faith? Well, let's look at Peter's words and consider the areas where we need to keep growing:

1. **Goodness.** Some translations use the term *virtue* or *moral goodness*. This means, essentially, that we need to keep our houses in order. We especially want to live free of secret sin, because secrets make us want to hide.

2. **Knowledge.** We should study God's Word privately and with our local churches. We don't just surrender our hearts to Jesus; we also surrender our minds.

3. **Self-control.** With the help of the Holy Spirit, Scripture, and the body of Christ, we are not controlled by our anger, our addiction, our lack of discipline, or our appetites.

4. **Endurance.** Life with Jesus is a long walk of obedience. We stay the course, we stay patient, and we don't give up.

5. **Godliness.** Lord willing, as we grow in all these ways, we look more and more like the One we love. Our lives bear evidence of His character because of how He is changing us.

6. **Brotherly affection.** We love our brothers and sisters in Christ like family. We believe the best about them. We honor them with our words and our actions.

7. **Love.** Our love for God and for mankind is ever increasing, and others see that love in us.

Even when don't feel close to God or we feel discouraged in our faith, the Lord is gracious and merciful. He will help us see what we can't, and He will give us what we do not have. Today is a great day to talk to the Lord and take inventory of these different parts of our lives. We want to be people who remember, so we need to be people who are growing. What kindness that He shows us the way!

READ 2 PETER 1:12–15.

1. Have you ever felt numb in your faith? Like you have knowledge in your head, but it's not affecting your heart? What shook you out of it? Or are you still in it? Explain that a little.

2. In verse 13, Peter says that he wants to "wake [us] up with a reminder." Why does it matter if believers are "awake," so to speak?

3. Of the seven areas Peter mentions in 2 Peter 1:5–7, which one presents the biggest struggle for you?

4. Who are a few trustworthy people who could pray for you about that area of struggle? How specifically do you need them to pray?

TODAY'S PRAYER

Day 25

J'm not sure if we're supposed to have favorites in this particular area, but Luke is my absolute favorite book of the Bible. I think it's because we see the full scope of Jesus' life on earth—birth, ministry, death, resurrection—so if we want to see what He was like and how He talked and all the ways He loved people, the book of Luke is like a one-stop shop. And now that I've written that last sentence, I realize that it doesn't sound super sophisticated in regard to Luke's importance, but I'm trusting you understand what I mean.

Thank you for your patience.

Ironically, one of the most memorable moments in Luke (for me) actually happened before Jesus arrived on the scene. It's shortly after His mother, Mary, found out she would be giving birth to, you know, the Savior of the world. She was (1) unmarried, (2) a virgin, and (3) around fourteen years old. She was understandably confused, and after taking a moment to respond to the angel Gabriel, who prophesied her pregnancy, she answered with resolve: "Behold, I am the servant of the Lord; let it be to me according to your word" (Luke 1:38 ESV).

I've read the passage about the proclamation of Mary's pregnancy and her subsequent trip to her cousin Elizabeth's house countless times (just FYI, that's not because I'm trying to set a record; it's because I wrote a book that focused on Mary and Elizabeth's relationship), but it was only a couple of years ago when two words jumped off the page at me like I'd never seen them before. They're in verse 39, right after Gabriel leaves Mary: "In those days Mary arose and went with haste into the hill country, to a town in Judah."

Do you see them? "Mary arose."

Listen. Those two words preach to me like crazy. Mary had just heard the most shocking news of her young life. She was no doubt overwhelmed, confused, and scared. She was uneducated, unmarried, and unable to provide for herself. But somehow, in the middle of all those feelings that could have figuratively knocked her down, Mary made a critical decision: She got up. She arose.

We know from Scripture that Mary specifically got up so she could go to her cousin Elizabeth's house. That was a great first step, because when she arrived, her cousin met her with support and confirmation and encouragement. In our lives, the circumstances will no doubt be different, but no matter what we're facing, we can recognize the wisdom of Mary's decision to get up. That decision enabled her to get to a safe place with a safe person. That decision enabled her to hear Elizabeth's wisdom. That decision enabled her to see the bigger picture of what the Lord was doing (see verses 46–56).

Whether we're dealing with a friendship that has fallen apart, an illness that we didn't anticipate, or a loss that takes our breath away, we absolutely need to process all the feelings that accompany our unexpected circumstances. But we also get to follow Mary's lead: we get to get up, and we get to trust that the Lord will lead us where we need to be.

READ PSALM 37:23–24.

1. What's the most unexpected news you have ever received? How did you respond?

_____

_____

_____

2. Have you ever thought about how Mary must have felt after she received Gabriel's news? What do you imagine it was like in those initial moments after she learned she would give birth to Jesus?

_____

_____

_____

3. Look up Luke 1:49. Write or doodle it here.

4. When we're dealing with a situation we weren't expecting, why is the simple act of getting up sometimes really hard?

TODAY'S PRAYER

Day 26

One of my favorite walking trails is about two-thirds flat, one-third hills, with a steep, long incline at the end that will make anyone feel a little bit like a champion when you reach the top. I don't celebrate and pump my fists in the air when I get there, but that's only because I typically need to put my hands on my knees and remember how to breathe again. That is to say: WHERE CAN I FIND MY GOLD MEDAL?

As someone who was born with the gift of clumsiness, I try to be super careful when I walk the trail because so many roots are exposed. There's one section in particular where I always slow down because the roots are such an obstacle. I don't mind it, though, because I feel like I'm walking a high wire (if said high wire were two inches off the ground). Over time I've figured out how to stay on the lookout for roots and rocks, so I now feel strangely agile on terrain that can be uncertain.

Last week I went to the trail for my usual Saturday morning walk, and after about twenty steps I realized the trail didn't feel the same under my feet. And as I continued to walk, I figured it out: the park staff had covered the trail in a fresh layer of gravel. It should have been a good thing; after all, there was an extra layer between the bottom of my feet and the ground. But on some level, I missed the bumps and the dips. I missed the drop-offs. I missed having to pay attention to where my foot landed when I skimmed over an exposed root. And after about a half mile, a thought occurred to me: *the level ground is almost disorienting.*

As I pondered this idea, I realized that the same is true in real life, especially on a spiritual level. We grow accustomed to uncertainty or drama or dysfunction or illness—circumstances that are constantly keeping us off-balance, causing us to tread carefully as we navigate them—and then, when there's finally a sense of resolution or healing or restoration or peace, we almost don't know what to do with ourselves. We've gotten so used to sidestepping roots and rocks that we aren't sure how to respond to level ground. Even in our relationship with the Lord, we can grow more comfortable with crying out to Him in panic and desperation as opposed to approaching Him in confidence and trust.

So here's what the trail reminded me. We will always navigate roots and rocks. We will always face uncertainty. But in Christ, our footing is always sure. It's easy to forget that when—and I'm speaking figuratively here—we're constantly battling bumpy terrain. So when we find ourselves in the middle of an easier, smoother path—when life has settled into a rhythm where we aren't quite as disrupted by the roots and rocks—*thanks be to God*. In *The Message*, Proverbs 12:3 says this: "You can't find firm footing in a swamp, but life rooted in God stands firm." He guides us and keeps us steady in times of calm and times of turmoil. We find our security in Him, not in what the road looks like.

Praise Him today for the fact that although our circumstances may change, He never does.

READ PSALM 143:8–10.

1. Can you think of a time when your life felt unsteady and uncertain? Explain.

_____

_____

_____

_____

2. Do you think we can sometimes grow accustomed—or even addicted—to the emotional roller coaster of drama and dysfunction? Why or why not?

_____

_____

_____

3. Do you feel relieved when life is less bumpy than normal? Or do you feel a little bored? Explain.

4. Write out the last sentence in verse 10 of Psalm 143.

TODAY'S PRAYER

Day 27

*N*ot too long ago my husband had a yearly checkup, and the doctor said something doctors have been known to say from time to time: *"You're doing great, but think about cutting back on saturated fats and sugar."* So my husband, being a good patient, decided to do just that.

For almost three months, David did exactly what his doctor suggested. Sure, for the first few days of no sugar, he felt terrible and *may* have been the tiniest bit grumpy, but after about a week, he felt great. He was sleeping better, had more energy, and was less hungry throughout the day. It was a win!

A few months into his new eating plan, though, he decided to give himself a cheat day on a holiday weekend. We've all probably done the same kind of thing after a period of trying to be healthier, and in a way, those cheat days feel like a reward. *I've done what the doctor asked! Now I will break all the rules!*

The morning of the Official Cheat Day, David woke up bright and early to get apple fritters at our favorite donut shop. Enjoying half a fritter for breakfast felt like a well-earned indulgence. Later we met friends for lunch, and the four of us sampled blueberry cobbler cheesecake, molten chocolate cake with ice cream, and key lime pie. Man-oh-man, we left feeling like we'd enjoyed the feast of our lives.

David and I ran a few errands after lunch, and when we got to our third stop, he was at a low ebb. After we got home, he plopped down in his chair and made a proclamation: "I. FEEL. TERRIBLE." The sugar had done him wrong even though it had seemed so right.

If left to pure logic, David would have told you that loading up a cheat day with so many sugary treats wasn't a great idea, but something in him thought he could test what he knew was true and somehow dodge any consequences. This same kind of reasoning has been true for, well, ALL OF HUMANITY. And although we're just talking about eating sugar when a doctor had said, *Hey, sugar isn't a great idea*, we can be guilty of this same kind of thinking when issues of more serious disobedience are on the table. Maybe we decide we're tired of being "the responsible one" and dabble in some reckless behavior. Maybe we make up our minds that a substance isn't as dangerous as people say and agree to try it. Maybe we're tired of fighting temptation and figure that as long as it stays secret, it's okay.

In Romans 7, Paul ponders this battle we all face—this tendency to go against what we know is right—when he writes, "For I do not do the good that I want to do, but I practice the evil that I do not want to do" (v. 19). Every decision has consequences, and before we commit to something unwise or unhealthy, it's helpful to (1) be honest with ourselves about the possible consequences, and (2) remember we serve a gracious, compassionate God who has told us what is right and good. And no matter what, we can give thanks that even when we make bad decisions, He is quick to forgive when we mess up and confess our sins.

Praise Him for His faithfulness today.

READ ROMANS 7:15–23,

1. What is a temptation you've recently faced? It doesn't have to be anything super serious (please see: apple fritters), but if it is, remember that God would never shame you for your struggle.

_____

_____

_____

2. Paul's words in the passage you read today initially sound a little bit like a riddle. If you were to summarize the verses in one sentence, what would you say?

_____

_____

_____

3. What's something you need to do but are having a hard time doing?

_____

_____

_____

4. When you do something you know you shouldn't have done, does that affect how you see yourself? How you engage with other people? How you interact with God? Explain that a little bit.

_____

_____

_____

TODAY'S PRAYER

_____

_____

_____

_____

_____

_____

_____

_____

_____

_____

_____

Day 28

*W*hen I was in college, I decided I really didn't like the way my upper arms looked. I don't know why I was so critical of my upper arms—I can't remember anyone ever criticizing them or pointing out their inferior qualities—but for some reason I made up my mind that I didn't want them on display. So no matter the temperature and no matter the season, I wore clothes with longer sleeves. Long-sleeve shirts, ¾-sleeve shirts, jackets, sweaters, you name it. Oh, I would sweat like crazy, but what mattered most was that my arms were covered.

I would love to tell you that this was a passing phase, but with the exception of a few years in my late twenties, I continued to tell myself that I needed to cover my arms. Basically this meant that for the better part of twenty-plus years, I spent every spring and summer burning up. I finally broke myself of this habit IN MY FORTIES when (1) I started exercising regularly, and (2) I had to let go of the preoccupation with my arms lest I have a heat stroke. So about five years ago, when I went to Target and bought a truly short-sleeved shirt—a cute tie-dye top that I planned to wear to work and church and other places outside of my house (can you even believe it?!)—I was a bit taken aback when I wore it for the first time and nobody seemed to feel offended by how the tops of my arms looked. The negative voice in my head had persisted for so long that I had lost my ability to realize it had been lying to me all along.

How about that?

This same thing happens in other areas of our lives. Maybe we believe a lie about our ability to be a good friend. Maybe we believe a lie that we're inherently unlovable. Maybe we believe the worst about someone else. Maybe we decide we could never do X, Y, or Z because we would surely embarrass ourselves or fail before we really got started. Maybe we believe that our comfort and peace can only be found in something illegal or immoral. Sometimes these false beliefs are rooted in events from our past, and sometimes they're seemingly random perceptions of ourselves that we've chosen to believe. Regardless, if we're going to live and walk in freedom, we have to ask the Lord to help us get untangled from our wrong thinking and/or our wrongdoing.

I don't know a formula for overcoming the lies we believe about ourselves, but I do know this: we can't fight what we're unwilling to identify. Sometimes we stay in certain patterns of unbelief or wrong belief for so long that they feel completely normal to us. So today is a great day to consider if some thoughts, feelings, or beliefs that boss you around contradict what God says in Scripture. Are there places in your head and heart where a lie has attempted to overtake the truth of who you are in Christ? That lie—whether big or small—has no hold on you and no authority over you. Reject it. Take some time today to remind yourself how deeply you're loved by Jesus (1 John 4:16), how completely His grace covers you (2 Corinthians 12:9), and how dependably the Holy Spirit leads us to freedom (2 Corinthians 3:17).

The Truth will set you free (John 8:32).

READ HEBREWS 12:1-3.

1. Can you identify any lie(s) you currently believe about yourself?

2. Do you have any idea how or when the lie(s) started to take hold of your head and your heart?

3. Does the lie have a tendency to make you feel weary (Hebrews 12:3)? How is that affecting your life? How do you think your life would change if you believed the truth?

_____

_____

_____

_____

4. Look up Psalm 139:14. Write/doodle/illustrate it here.

_____

_____

_____

_____

TODAY'S PRAYER

_____

_____

_____

_____

_____

_____

_____

_____

_____

Day 29

$\mathcal{S}$ince our dog, Hazel, gets dialed all the way up with anxiety when, you know, the garbage truck comes by on Monday mornings, you can imagine how NOT AT ALL relaxed she is when it's time for her to go to the vet and have an assortment of people come in and out of the room to take her blood and check her eyes and—woe be unto the vet techs—give her shots.

Last week I took Hazel in for her annual checkup, and even though the people at the vet clinic take excellent care of her, she was a nervous wreck from the time I pulled into the parking lot. I lifted her out of the car and took her on a little walk around the perimeter of the building; I thought maybe moving around would calm her down a bit. Sure enough, after about thirty seconds of exploring, Hazel seemed to have calmed down to a point of slight nervousness instead of the full-blown, white-hot panic of just a few minutes earlier.

However, even though Hazel was calmer, I noticed one big difference from how she normally behaves: she was constantly looking in my direction. If we took a step to the left, she looked up to make sure I was still there. If we walked straight ahead, she would turn her head toward me every few seconds, almost like she needed to check in. After we went inside, it was the same deal: she was constantly making eye contact with me, never letting me out of her sight, and doing everything in her power to stay ridiculously close to me as I filled out the paperwork.

When it was time for Hazel to go to the back for her checkup, she responded better than I expected. And while she willingly followed the technician who was taking her to the treatment room, she continued to turn and look at me. In a situation with some uncertainty, I was Hazel's Human Security Blanket, and as long as I was in her line of vision, she remained (relatively) calm.

This is where I feel like Hazel might be able to teach us a few things. Because as we come up against situations that cause anxiety or panic or whatever kind of emotional discomfort, we will do well to continue to look to Jesus—to keep Him in our line of sight at all times. We can do this through prayer or reading Scripture or meeting with a mentor who encourages us to remember the ultimate Source of our security. No matter what kind of circumstances we're navigating—and no matter how nervous or unsteady we might feel—we fix our eyes on Jesus. We stay close to Him. We look to Him as often as necessary so that we can rest in the peace of knowing that He is with us, He is for us, and He will never abandon us. He might not walk us around a parking lot (I promise I'm smiling), but He will be sure and steady when life feels like anything but.

Thank Jesus today for His faithfulness—because every single time you look to Him in the middle of uncertainty, He is there. He will never leave your side.

READ PSALM 121:1–8.

1. When was the last time you felt legitimately afraid? How did you handle your fear?

_____

_____

_____

_____

2. Is there a person in your life who makes you feel more secure just by being near you? Explain a little bit.

_____

_____

_____

_____

3. What are some things that remind you of your security in Jesus? Do you have a few favorite verses of Scripture? Or a hymn or worship song you really love?

4. Look up the lyrics to "Turn Your Eyes Upon Jesus." Pick the stanza that speaks to you the most and write it out here.

TODAY'S PRAYER

Day 30

*M*y coworker and friend Heather recently told me a story her daughter, Caroline, had told her. Earlier this week Caroline was lunching outside with a group of her fellow seniors, and one of Caroline's friends (we'll call her Emma) mentioned that her car—which was next to where they were sitting—was absolutely filthy inside. I didn't get the full rundown on why the inside of Emma's car was in less-than-stellar condition, but the gist was that it had seen better days: lots of random clothing items and fast-food napkins and stuff she needed to return to friends or take inside her house or whatever. And although the mess probably wasn't overwhelming initially, Emma had officially reached the point of *Oh my goodness—I don't want to live like this anymore.*

What happened next continues to make me smile. Someone in the lunch group said, "You know what? We can help with that right now!" And before Emma knew it, her jump-to-it friend had run across the parking lot to grab a trash can. He wheeled it over to Emma's car, and within minutes, that group of seniors was TAKING CARE OF BUSINESS. They opened the doors and the trunk and started sorting through the junk. They threw away trash, stacked and folded clothes, figured out what needed to be returned where, and over the course of twenty minutes, got that car situation HANDLED. What had been overwhelming to Emma for the better part of a few weeks was fairly light work after her friends got involved. And by the end of lunch, the inside of Emma's car only needed a quick vacuum when she got home from school.

I know this is such a simple, everyday example, but it's still a great, practical picture of how healthy Christian community should operate. Emma was feeling burdened by something she was trying (and failing) to manage on her own, she acknowledged that burden to trusted friends, and her friends immediately came alongside to support her. I realize that in this case we're talking about a car interior in need of some TLC, but the same response would apply in a more serious situation . . . like if a childhood friend admits she's in an unhealthy relationship, or your college roommate confesses she's battling an addiction, or a coworker tells you over lunch that she's weary from fighting a chronic illness. When we truly love our neighbors, helping one another is an all-hands-on-deck event.

Here's what's important too: Emma not only admitted she was overwhelmed, but she also took responsibility for her part in the mess. She unlocked the car so others could see what was going on, and she helped with the clean-out. Granted, sometimes the people who are struggling can't participate in their community's efforts to help, but when they can—and when they do—it's almost always an encouraging sign that they're humbly and sincerely willing to link arms and walk toward healing with others. "Healing" being a strong word for a backseat full of fast-food napkins, of course, but I think you know what I mean.

Love your people well today—and let them love you too. Jesus wouldn't have it any other way.

READ JOHN 13:34–35.

1. When was the last time you opened up to someone about a literal or figurative mess in your life?

_____

_____

_____

_____

2. Why can it sometimes be overwhelming to let a trusted friend know about something difficult you're facing? Why do you think it can be hard for us to let people see what's really going on?

_____

_____

_____

3. Look up Luke 6:31. Write/doodle/illustrate it here.

4. Is it easy for you to notice when other people need your help? How do you respond in those kinds of situations?

TODAY'S PRAYER

Day 31

We know that Scripture is filled with words that are God-breathed and eternally true. But every once in a while, a certain verse resonates in our heart and our mind in a unique way. For me one of those verses is Colossians 3:4, which contains five words that are an instant perspective shifter in the middle of the challenges of the day-to-day: "Christ, who is your life."

Christ is my life.

Christ is your life.

And here's what that means for you and for me.

Our reputation is not our life.

Our family background is not our life.

Our academic standing is not our life.

Our professional success is not our life.

Our achievement is not our life.

Our friend group is not our life.

Our neighborhood is not our life.

Our church is not our life.

Our religion is not our life.

Our frustration is not our life.

Our disappointment is not our life.

Our failure is not our life.

Our bank account is not our life.

Our relationship status is not our life.

Our heartache is not our life.

Our past is not our life.

Our fear is not our life.

Our carefully constructed image is not our life.

Our athletic ability is not our life.

Our people pleasing is not our life.

Our rule keeping is not our life.

Our rule breaking is not our life.

Our political party is not our life.

Our perfectionism is not our life.

Our apathy is not our life.

Jesus Christ—the "King eternal, immortal, invisible, the only God" (1 Timothy 1:17)—He is our life.

Rest in that grace today.

Amen.

READ PHILIPPIANS 3:7–9.

1. What are a few things that tend to make you forget that Christ is your life? Worry? The desire for someone's approval? A preoccupation with your image? Something else?

2. When do you rest most securely in who Jesus is? When are you most likely to remember that He is, in fact, your life? Maybe it's when you worship, or when you're outside, or when you have the opportunity to have genuine conversations about Him. Write down whatever it is, and explain that a bit.

3. Sit for a few moments and think about the fact that Christ is your life. What does that mean? What does that change?

4. How can you remind yourself today that Christ is your life? A sticky note in your car? A message on your mirror? A reminder that pops up on your phone? Do two or three tangible things that will bring your mind back to the truth that Christ is your life.

TODAY'S PRAYER

Day 32

*F*or years I've heard people describe times of intense communion and intimacy with Jesus as "mountaintop experiences." I've heard that phrase so frequently that I'm tempted to write Mountaintop Experiences—because it is A WHOLE THING with Christians. There's something about that mountaintop feeling that makes us think we are destined to live the rest of our lives as spiritual champions (excuse me, Spiritual Champions), that we'll share the gospel and lead people to Jesus on a daily basis, and that our spiritual fire, as it were, will therefore never burn out.

However.

Real life isn't confined to a mountaintop. And as we navigate the ups and downs of life, we'll spend time in our fair share of valleys. Now, it's true we can experience joy and contentment in either place—the mountaintop or the valley—but for me, at least, the perception that I've spent too much time in a valley can leave me with a little something I like to refer to as the spiritual blahs.

The truth of the matter is that we can love Jesus with our whole heart and still feel spiritually lethargic at times. We can feel unmotivated, we can feel overwhelmed, and we can even feel distant from the One who has so graciously and sacrificially paid the price for every single one of our sins.

But as someone who has walked with the Lord for a while—over many a mountain and through many a valley—here's what I know: God mercifully uses the valleys to graciously draw us even closer to Himself. In fact, when I look back over the long and winding road of my spiritual life, I can see how God has used spiritual valleys to settle something significant in my relationship with Him. Even the last ten years testify to this. Back in 2013, it was fear. In 2016, it was apathy. In 2018, it was anger.

And here's what I know: no matter how exhilarating the mountains are, there will always be valleys. In fact, as I heard a friend say recently, "The valleys are where real life happens." So when I find myself in a place of spiritual blahs, I will ask the Lord to help me do three things:

1. Remember who He is and how faithfully He has cared for me.

2. Fight isolation by consistently meeting and praying with Christian community.

3. Turn to Scripture for answers, encouragement, and the whole Truth (this means I refuse to listen to my fickle and temperamental heart).

A spiritual mountaintop is invigorating, no doubt about it. But don't discount the good work the Lord does in the valleys. By His grace, He loves us, teaches us, changes us, and strengthens us in the highs *and* the lows. What a Savior!

READ ISAIAH 40:1–5.

1. When was the last time you felt like you were walking on a mountaintop with the Lord? When you were energized, encouraged, and renewed in your relationship with Him?

_____

_____

_____

_____

2. When was the last time you felt "blah" spiritually? Explain.

_____

_____

_____

_____

3. When you're in a low place spiritually, how does that affect the rest of your life? Can you see the impact of the valley in your relationships? Your choices? Your confidence?

4. Reread Isaiah 40:3–5. Do those verses comfort you? What do they ultimately reveal about mountaintops and valleys?

TODAY'S PRAYER

Day 33

A while back, I flew on an airplane for the first time in almost a year. All of us witnessed the world turning upside down with so many people battling COVID-19, and as I sat in the Atlanta airport waiting on my flight, I thought about how strange it was to see everyone moving through the terminal wearing masks. It was a completely different experience than not even a year before.

And even though it may sound super odd to say what I'm about to say, I'm going to say it anyway: the persistent sight of people wearing masks made me think a whole lot about sin.

Yes. You read that correctly. *Sin.*

Here's what I mean. The virus that causes COVID is invisible; we can sit in its presence and have absolutely no idea. And if we catch the virus, it can manifest in a myriad of ways—from very mild symptoms to death. It's the same with sin that has made itself at home in our hearts or our minds. It's mostly invisible to the naked eye (though certainly, like with COVID, we can show symptoms), but the consequences of that sin can range from minor discomfort to full-blown devastation. And just like there are certain precautions we need to take to protect ourselves (and our neighbors!) from COVID, there are also precautions we need to take when it comes to guarding against "the sin that so easily ensnares us" (Hebrews 12:1).

Below are three things I hope will encourage us as we fight the good fight against sin today. The irony is that these recommendations are markedly different than what we saw with the COVID pandemic. But different battles require different tactics, right?

1. **Stay out of quarantine.** Our sin can drive us into a personal lockdown of sorts because we're ashamed, we fear judgment, or we assume no one will understand our particular struggle. Here's what I want to tell you about that philosophy: it's a lie. Sin grows in isolation, and it loves the dark. That's all the more reason to make sure you're not hiding from others.

2. **Avoid social distancing.** When it comes to sin, it's great to take yourself out of quarantine, and it's even better to commit to ongoing, safe Christian community. Maybe you join a small group at your church, or maybe you study the Bible with a few close friends every week, or maybe there's an older woman in your church you chat with twice a month. You don't have to stand in front of the church and proclaim, "I HAVE SIGNIFICANT ISSUES WITH ENVY AND RESENTMENT." You just need one or two people to listen, love you right where you are, remind you who you are in Christ, and pray with you.

3. **Don't wear a mask.** When you're struggling with something, it can be oh-so-tempting to slap on a (figurative) mask and pretend like everything is oh-so-fine. When you do that, though, you often miss the grace that's just on the other side of honesty. The Lord wants to love you through His Word and His people. You don't have to hide your struggle. You don't have to mask your sin. Your real life is beautiful.

Remember this today: you are loved.

READ ROMANS 6:12–14.

1. What are some struggles in your head or your heart that make you want to hide?

_____

_____

2. Can you think of a time when you really needed encouragement and truth from other people, but you isolated yourself instead? Why do you think you did that?

_____

_____

3. Right now—on this very day you're working through this devotional—what person or people feel like your most dependable, honest community? If you can't think of anyone, then think of where you might go to find it.

4. Look up the hymn "Come Thou Fount of Every Blessing." Write out the fourth verse here.

TODAY'S PRAYER

Day 34

*A*s neighborhoods go, ours is a pretty active one. No matter what time of day, you're bound to see people walking their dogs, hiking, playing tennis, or riding bikes. It's comforting, the level of activity, because it always reminds me that real life is happening all around us.

Over the years, though, one regular exerciser stands out to me no matter the season. This man walks every single day, and he always wears heavy layers of clothing. I've noticed because when it is August in Alabama, even a pair of shorts with a T-shirt can feel like an oppressive amount of clothes. So to repeatedly see someone who is always wearing track pants and sometimes two sweatshirts—well, it stands out. I'm sure he has his own good reasons for dressing the way he does, but just the sight of him makes me want to blast the A/C in my car. He no doubt gets a great workout, but man alive, he has to be burning up, even when it's cold outside.

One warm September day I saw the man on his afternoon walk, and as I pondered wearing all those layers, I thought about how I can do the exact same thing—only I'm weighing myself down on an emotional and spiritual level. I pile on layers of resentment or bitterness or shame. Instead of clothing myself in "strength and honor" (Proverbs 31:25), I might decide instead to let anger and self-righteousness be my outfit of the day. Sure, we are all multi-dimensional people with lots of elements and shades to our personalities, but we might find ourselves choosing spiritual and emotional clothing that is way too heavy. We may think that it makes us stronger, but the reality could well be that it ultimately slows us down.

Of course the man in my neighborhood can dress however he wants when he heads out on his daily walks. If he wants to wear twenty-eight T-shirts, more power to him. But when it comes to the emotional and spiritual parts of our lives, we need to take regular inventory of our burdens. Dealing with the burden might not be as simple as taking off an extra sweatshirt, but we might be surprised by how working through that issue helps us walk in more freedom. We might be surprised by how getting rid of it lightens our load.

Be mindful today that at any point when an emotional or spiritual struggle feels like it's weighing you down, you get to take that thing straight to Jesus. You can't literally remove it from your heart, of course, but you can say this: "Jesus, _____ is too heavy for me to carry today, and I am tired. I know You are the lifter of my burdens, so I ask You to help me bear _____ with wisdom. Help me to think about it like You think about it. Show me how to walk with You in a way that _____ doesn't hinder me or slow me down. I trust You with _____, and I know You can handle it. May You get great glory as I work through it. In Your name I pray. Amen."

Walk a little lighter today. Jesus can carry what you can't.

READ ISAIAH 58:6–8.

1. Is there anything that's currently weighing you down? Stress? Sadness? Something else?

_____

_____

_____

_____

2. What are you carrying unnecessarily? Have you taken on someone else's problems? Or are you holding on to guilt about something when the Lord forgave you years ago? Think about that for a few minutes before you write your answer.

_____

_____

_____

_____

3. Is there a particular area of your life where you tend to carry more than you have to? School? Work? Family stuff? Why do you think you do that? Who are you trying to please?

4. Do you think you live like someone who is free in Christ? Why or why not?

TODAY'S PRAYER

Day 35

The amount of information we take in every day is staggering. From the time we wake up in the morning until we go to bed at night, we are inundated with opinions and forecasts and hot takes. We're listening to music and catching up on messages and scrolling through our phones. We're passing along memes and tweets and GIFs throughout our day—maybe even while we're reading or binging our latest favorite show—and it's likely that until we lie down to go to sleep, our phone has basically been a persistent, three-by-six-inch boss: chirping at us, notifying us, asking us questions, and reminding us where we're supposed to be.

We've grown so accustomed to incessant information consumption that we have built up an enormous tolerance for the constant noise and interruptions and demands; and the irony is that if we had a friend who tapped us on the shoulder fifty or sixty times a day to tell us what we needed to think about or listen to or do, we would likely ask that friend to BACK OFF in pretty short order.

It's unlikely that most of us will figure out a way to completely disentangle ourselves from the persistent buzz of devices and social media. But what we *can* do is intentionally set aside time to create instead of consume. We love and serve a creative God who has made us to be creative people. That doesn't mean you have to paint a museum-quality painting or produce an independent film. It just means you can honor the Lord by offering your creativity.

And here's the thing: creativity doesn't need to be complicated. Maybe you learn to make your grandmother's pound cake; maybe you rearrange your bedroom in a way that feels comforting and beautiful; maybe you journal about something God has been teaching you. You could plant a container vegetable garden or create an arrangement for the dining room table out of greenery from around your house. You could even write a letter to an elderly relative who needs encouragement. The point isn't to do something elaborate; the point is to contribute to the beauty and the health of your little corner of the world by exercising your creative gifts—gifts that reflect the heart, the grace, and the generosity of our Savior.

So today, if you're tempted to numb out by watching one or four and a half hours of the latest video content, consider how you might create instead of consume. Consider how you might shine some light. The gifts the Lord has given you are meant to be shared, not so that you will receive lots of pats on the back and positive affirmation, but so that others might see Him in the things you create. Yes, the world seems to place a high value on grand gestures and viral fame and public recognition, but your humble, simple act of creativity could make a real difference in someone's life. Your willingness to create—and even to inspire—will not only provide rest for your heart and mind, but it could very well remind someone of the love and care of their heavenly Father.

Your creative efforts may seem small, but they hold great purpose. Make something beautiful today.

READ AMOS 4:13.

1. What are some of your favorite creative outlets? Do you like to build things? Draw? Sing? List three or four things that help your mind and your heart relax.

2. How much time do you dedicate to your favorite creative activities during an average week? Does that feel like enough to you?

3. Why do you think consumption can be so much more appealing than creativity? Why do we consume so much more content than we create?

_____

_____

_____

4. Think of one thing you would like to create today. How could that creativity be an act of worship or service to God?

_____

_____

_____

_____

TODAY'S PRAYER

_____

_____

_____

_____

_____

_____

_____

_____

_____

_____

Day 36

$\mathcal{F}$or the first, oh, *four decades* of my life, I was not an outdoorsy person. I didn't like activities that required "spending time in nature" or "losing access to air conditioning." I preferred to be inside, preferably with access to a television and a thermostat, thank you very much.

Over the last several years, though, I've experienced a gradual, unexpected shift: I now LOVE to be outside. In fact, if I don't have enough time outside over the course of a few days, I can get a little ornery. The best way I know to explain it is that being outside feels like a reset for my head and my heart—a different and needed way of experiencing the goodness of God—and I crave it way down deep in my bones.

An extension of my newly discovered outdoorsy enjoyment is that I've started to go hiking—like, in the woods and stuff. I don't want to overstate it, but if there had been a Least Likely to Hike award when I was in high school, I would have won a trophy *and* a crown. But now I'm such a fan. I love the way the pine straw crunches under my feet, the sense that I'm setting out on an adventure, and the feeling of being sheltered by the treetops. I'm ridiculously fond of the whole experience.

A couple of weeks ago my friend Heather and I went hiking at a state park. Heather is a much more skilled and knowledgeable hiker than I am, so I was excited to follow her down one of the trails and hopefully learn a thing or two as we enjoyed exploring God's creation. The trail was pretty wide, but I quickly noticed a lot of exposed roots. I usually try to carefully navigate roots that might pose a threat to my balance or my pace, but about a quarter mile into our hike, Heather said something that has stayed with me ever since: "I always like to step on a root—because if I don't, I underestimate what it takes to step over it, and then I trip or stumble."

I'm not sure if this is the official term or not, but I believe that's what you would call a Truth Bomb.

I mean, yes. Sure. It applies to hiking. But oh my goodness—isn't that also how we should deal with sin in our lives? So many times I have found myself facing temptation of one sort or another, and instead of stepping on it—getting it underfoot—I've tried to dodge it, hop over it, or even ignore it like it wasn't there. Those strategies may have worked for a while, but eventually that temptation tripped me up again. Sometimes I've been quick to regain my balance, but other times I've fallen flat on my face—or, even worse, been left with something broken that takes a long time to heal.

When you see something in your path that could potentially cause you to fall, ask the Lord to help you (figuratively, of course) step on it. Ask Him to help you notice the things that might trip you up. There's always grace, of course, when we fail and fall. But there's also grace in being wise about what's ahead and carefully watching where we walk. He is with you every step of the way.

READ ROMANS 8:12–17.

1. Be completely candid: is there something that's threatening to trip you up right now? An apology you need to give? A habit you need to break? A relationship you need to end?

_____

_____

_____

_____

2. If you think about stepping on that thing—instead of stepping over it—what would that take? What boundaries would you need to set for yourself?

_____

_____

_____

_____

3. Have you ever been in a situation where something tripped you up and you weren't even expecting it? How did you handle it?

4. What lessons have you learned from the stuff that has tripped you up in the past? What has the Lord taught you?

TODAY'S PRAYER

Day 37

*O*ne of my favorite things about working with teen girls is that I get to know them over a span of years, sometimes from seventh grade to twelfth grade. A life of faith is filled with highs, lows, and everything in between, and it has been a privilege to witness those moments and hear about them from my younger sisters in Christ. I don't take a single one of those conversations for granted.

Recently, I was thinking about a particularly difficult friendship situation I helped a girl navigate when she was a freshman (and when I say "helped," what I really mean is that I listened to her). Four years later, that situation is different in all sorts of wonderful ways. The Lord has changed hearts and mended hurts and provided real, deep understanding that has led to real, deep confession and repentance. And now, in the winter of her senior year, this girl can enjoy a beautiful, healthy relationship where there once was only a big ole pile of ashes. Covered in tears, no less.

Here's the deal: at this point the girl has forgotten some of the heartache from her freshman year. Now that her broken-down friendship is repaired, she doesn't think much about how hard it used to be. But every once in a while, when we're catching up about big stuff or little stuff and she casually mentions the name of that friend, I'll say, "Hey . . . remember? Remember when it wasn't so easy? Things are so good now! Look at the Lord!"

And inevitably she'll pause for a second, grin, and say, "Look at the Lord, Mrs. Soph!" Then we'll go right back to our conversation.

Given that, I want to make a point to say this—and I want to remember it for myself, as well—it is so good (SO! GOOD!) for us to process the challenges in our lives with other women who love Jesus. It's especially good for us to process those challenges with older women who love Jesus. Three quick reasons:

1. We can be reminded that the way it was isn't how it still is. The Lord changes things!

2. We can be reminded of specific ways we've seen God at work in our lives. The Lord heals what is broken!

3. We can be reminded that the credit for any healing does not belong to us. The Lord accomplishes what seems impossible!

So often we want our circumstances to change instantly; we want a quick fix with minimum inconvenience, especially in our relationships. But think about this: ships turn slowly. And many times the Lord moves us little bit by little bit, changing our direction so gradually that we don't always realize how He is orchestrating big changes. It's a help and a comfort to have someone in our lives who is witnessing the Lord's work, so that one day, when He has completely reoriented us in a relationship or a career or a passion, the other person can survey the new territory with us and boldly declare what we know to be true: "Look at the Lord!"

He will do it. Just give Him time.

READ PSALM 40:1–5.

1. Can you think of a relationship or a situation in your life that is very different than it was four or five years ago?

_____

_____

_____

_____

2. What caused the circumstances to change? Did the change happen quickly? Were the changes for good?

_____

_____

_____

3. Is there a trustworthy older person who gets an up close look at what is going on in your life? If yes, explain—and if not, write about why that might be helpful.

_____

_____

_____

4. Why is it helpful to have someone else's perspective when it comes to big events or big changes in your life?

_____

_____

_____

TODAY'S PRAYER

_____

_____

_____

_____

_____

_____

_____

_____

_____

_____

_____

_____

Day 38

A friend of mine who is a high school teacher told me a story recently, and when I realized I was still thinking about it three days later, I asked my friend if I could share it with you. She was kind enough to say yes.

Like so many teachers, my friend worked on campus during the COVID pandemic and had to enforce her school's policies about masks. Her school required everyone on campus to wear masks when changing classes, and there were specifications about what kinds of masks: how they were made, how they were worn, and what they could and couldn't say. You can file this in the "Things No One Even Knew to Think About Two Years Ago" folder.

Well. One day my teacher friend saw one of her students walking down the hall and noticed that the student's mask wasn't allowed because it promoted a political candidate. My friend turned away to handle some other pressing matter, making a mental note to address that student when he got to her classroom. A couple of minutes later, my friend started to walk toward the student's desk, wondering if the mask conversation was going to be uncomfortable or tense. But as soon as she saw her student's face, she realized he had changed into another mask, one that was appropriate for the classroom and within school guidelines.

He had put on a mask that worked for that particular situation. Figuratively, at least, so many of us do the same thing.

When I was growing up, I felt like I had about seven different versions of my personality: one for home, one for school, one for youth group, one for dance class, and on and on and on. It wasn't that I was trying to be fake; I just knew how to add to or subtract from my personality so that I blended in with the crowd (and gained acceptance) as easily as possible. Now that I'm older, I can occasionally fall into the same pattern if I'm in a situation where I feel insecure or vulnerable. At work I often see students wrestle with the temptation to "change masks," so to speak; they alter how they present themselves or interact with others when they fear being left out or want desperately to be noticed.

At some point we've all likely sacrificed who we really are and who God made us to be on the altar of someone's approval or acceptance. But constantly switching masks is an exhausting way to live. (Ask me how I know.)

My friend and fellow author Jamie Ivey wrote a book titled *You Be You*. Take her wise advice, and choose to be you. Remember today that God made you with great intention, with specific gifts, and with unconditional acceptance in His kingdom. Instead of swapping one identity for another as you move throughout your day, trust completely in your identity in Christ, which is sealed and secure. It definitely beats swapping masks all day long.

You are one of a kind. And no matter where you are or what you're doing, Christ in you is more than enough.

READ JEREMIAH 17:7–8.

1. What are three adjectives you would use to describe yourself at this point in your life?

_____

_____

_____

_____

2. Do you feel at peace not just with who you are but with how God made you? Why or why not?

_____

_____

_____

_____

3. In what kinds of situations are you most tempted to put on a different mask, so to speak? At school? At social gatherings? When you're with a new group of people? Write about that a little bit.

4. Are there places or situations where you know you don't have to wear a mask at all? Where you are free to be completely yourself? Explain.

TODAY'S PRAYER

Day 39

Jf we're honest—and I hope we will be, because this page right here is a safe place—then it probably wouldn't take us long to make a list of hypothetical situations that make us feel powerful or in control of our lives.

Here. I'll start.

- Achieving something we think will make us stand out from the crowd
- Being accepted into a particular group of friends
- Receiving interest or attention from a longtime crush
- Making a last-second goal to win the championship game
- Being validated as "right" on a controversial issue
- Seeing someone held publicly accountable for wrongdoing
- Earning a certain level of financial success
- Having enough influence at school or in an organization to move our agenda forward or shut down someone else's

And that's just the tip of the iceberg, right? Because all too often, when life feels out of our control, we script an alternate reality in our heads, a place where we dictate the circumstances, the players, and the outcome. Even though it might not be our intention, when we sink deep into our preferred version of "reality," our functioning hope rests in an imagined world where we only win, we only dominate, and we only succeed. After all, if we can control it, we want to win. Losing is for suckers, right?

Well. Not exactly.

Scripture reminds us over and over that our hope isn't in achievements or recognition or power. Those things occasionally feel great in a world that has conditioned us to lean on them more than we should. But no matter how frustrating or even bleak our day-to-day might seem, the words of a hymn written in 1834 ring as true as ever:

My hope is built on nothing less
Than Jesus' blood and righteousness.
I dare not trust the sweetest frame
But wholly lean on Jesus' name.

No power compares to the hope we have in Him. No victory. No control. No imagined scenario that rivals the ending of an Oscar-winning movie. Yes, it sometimes feels like relief to escape to a pretend world where everything works out just like we want it to, but we have to remember that we're steeping our souls in false hope if we think anything other than Jesus can sustain us.

It's a phrase worth repeating: if He is all we have, we have all we need. Cling to the hope you have in Him today. It holds.

READ EPHESIANS 1:7–10.

1. What's a situation that's frustrating you right now? Something where you would love to be able to script how it works out, but you have to rest in hope instead?

_____

_____

_____

_____

2. What would it look like for you to trust Jesus with that situation today? Explain.

_____

_____

_____

_____

3. Look up the hymn "My Hope Is Built on Nothing Less." Write out the refrain.

_____

_____

_____

4. Where are you tempted to put your hope? In power? Notoriety? Recognition? Relationships? Something else?

_____

_____

_____

TODAY'S PRAYER

_____

_____

_____

_____

_____

_____

_____

_____

_____

_____

_____

Day 40

I grew up in a church where we recited the Lord's Prayer every single Sunday during our worship services. So, by the time I was two or three years old, I could say the whole prayer from memory, even if the words didn't totally make sense to me. I mean, I wasn't even in preschool yet, so the whole notion of "trespasses" was a little foggy, but it was clear to me that the Lord's Prayer was a time for everyone in the pews to acknowledge their sin together—and to acknowledge their need for God's help. Even at a young age, I found this to be a comforting practice.

Now that I'm all grown up, I'm a member of a church where we don't recite the Lord's Prayer each week. I haven't given much thought to it, honestly, but earlier this year, I was taken aback during my quiet time one morning. Real life was weighing heavy on my heart when I opened my Bible to my daily reading, which happened to be the Lord's Prayer. However, since my Bible is a different translation than what I grew up reciting, the words were slightly unfamiliar. I've always said, "Our Father, who art in heaven, hallowed be thy name," but the Christian Standard Bible (csb) says this (Matthew 6:9):

> "Our father in heaven,
> your name be honored as holy."

Isn't that beautiful? And doesn't that very short, very simple verse have the potential to alter our perspectives every single day?

When we don't understand why a certain situation in our family is so hard—

"Our father in heaven, your name be honored as holy."

When we're filled with indescribable peace and joy—

"Our father in heaven, your name be honored as holy."

When we're struggling with tension or conflict in a friendship—

"Our father in heaven, your name be honored as holy."

When we need strength and wisdom to do the next right thing—

"Our father in heaven, your name be honored as holy."

Those ten simple words remind us that, as believers, our first priority is to honor God—to consider His holiness before all and above all—and to ask Him to help us surrender our hearts in every situation we face.

His Kingdom come.
His will be done.
On earth as it is in heaven.

READ MATTHEW 6:9–14.

1. What's the first hymn or prayer you remember knowing from memory when you were younger? Write it out here.

_____

_____

_____

2. Do those words mean something different to you now than they did then? Explain.

_____

_____

_____

3. What's one practical way you can honor the Lord's name as holy today? With your words? With your thoughts? Something else?

4. On your favorite Bible app, look up today's passage from the CSB and read it out loud. Does a different translation affect how you listen to the words?

TODAY'S PRAYER

Day 41

*W*hen I was in junior high, I would use my dual-cassette boom box (snazzy!) (what's up, eighties?) to make tapes of my favorite songs. Eventually I moved into burning mixtape CDs on my Mac, and now I (still!) love to make playlists in my beloved Apple Music (no worries if you're a Spotify person; we can still be friends).

Recently a friend asked me how I find songs for my playlists, and my response was simple: Apple Music knows me well. I don't pretend to understand how the algorithms work, but based on how much information I have provided my Apple friends in terms of what I listen to and add to my library, I think it's safe to say that Apple Music's understanding of my musical taste is spot-on. More often than not its suggestions for songs I might like are on the money, and there have been countless times when I've listened to my weekly music recommendations and sighed with the contentment of feeling understood.

Soon after that conversation with my friend, it occurred to me that as much as I may feel like my favorite music app really knows me, that cannot compare to how I am known by my Father in heaven—how we are *all* known by Him. He made us, after all. He knows our thoughts and our worries and our sins and our struggles. He knows our joys and our gifts and our frustrations and our sorrows. He knows our mistakes and our successes and our idols and our compromises. There is not one detail of our lives that has escaped His awareness, His attention, or His care.

Granted, it might feel like a hard left to start off talking about mixtapes and then make a leap to the omniscience of Jesus. But if we find some small degree of comfort in being known by our music service or our streaming TV provider or the ads that pop up when we scroll social media, then the peace and joy that come from being completely known and completely loved by the Creator of the universe have to be downright awe-inspiring. We don't have to run or hide or pretend. We don't have to manipulate or control or persuade. That kind of acceptance from our heavenly Father— that level of knowing from our Savior—is grace upon grace for sure.

That doesn't mean, of course, that we sit in our sin, stubborn and unrepentant, but content to be known. That doesn't mean that we do whatever we want, whenever we want regardless of the consequences. But it does mean that when we turn to the Lord, when we acknowledge the places where we're wandering, when we ask Him for guidance and wisdom, His conviction and direction will be trustworthy and sure because He knows us inside and out. He made us with great purpose and intention. And He will never lead us astray because He is always pointing us to redemption, to health, and to healing.

Rest in the love, the care, and the deep knowing of Jesus today. His love for you is constant. His love for you is endless.

READ PSALM 139:13–18.

1. In terms of human people (I'm grinning), who knows you better than anyone else?

2. Is being really and truly known by someone a comfort to you? Or does it bother you sometimes?

3. Is it difficult for you to let people see what's going on with you way deep down? Explain.

_____

_____

_____

_____

4. Is there any area of your life where you've been trying to hide from God? Any area where you haven't fully trusted Him? Take some time to confess that today and ask for His wisdom and direction.

_____

_____

_____

_____

TODAY'S PRAYER

_____

_____

_____

_____

_____

_____

_____

_____

_____

_____

Day 42

When I was in college, a friend of mine always felt tempted to roll her eyes when someone said, "I had the strangest dream last night." She dreaded the inevitable attempts to interpret what it all meant, and she didn't want to hear details of someone walking through their elementary school, only it was really a gas station, and by the way, all of this took place on the moon.

I totally understood my friend's frustration. It can be difficult to make sense of someone else's subconscious, of course, but as someone who has spent most of her adult life trying to figure out a dream from my twenties that featured Jesus' return, my parents' pasture, and a Volkswagen Bug, I can't deny my fascination with the stuff our minds process while we're sleeping.

Not too long ago, in fact, I woke up in the middle of the night, filled with emotion over a dream. I'll spare you the details (my college friend would be super proud of me for this), but the last part I remember was walking into my parents' room in my childhood home. While I couldn't quite make out who was sitting in a rocking chair in the corner, I knew as soon as she said my name that it was my mama.

Some backstory might be helpful. My mama died about five years ago, and even though I miss so many things about her, the sound of her voice is near the top of the list. From the time I went to college until the last year of her life, we talked on the phone several times a week, and the tone of her voice—the cadence of her words, even—was a constant in my life. Now that she's in heaven, I rejoice in knowing she's with Jesus, but there are still times when I would give anything just to sit and talk with her.

Maybe that's part of the reason my dream made me so emotional—because I still miss my mama like crazy. The more I lay in bed and thought about it, though, the more I felt strangely comforted by my dream. I couldn't see her face—and I couldn't touch her—but I still knew the sound of her voice.

Something about that realization made my heart swell with joy. And for the rest of the day, I continued to think about the gift of recognizing the sound of Mama's voice. It's a testimony to the affection and care I associate with my mama, to the years she sacrificially poured into my life. I might not be able to see her face-to-face, but the sound of her voice lives on in my heart and my memories. I'm deeply grateful for that.

Our relationships with the Lord operate in a similar way. We cannot see His face this side of heaven, but by His grace, we know His voice. It is just as familiar to us as the friend we sit with in English class, as the grandparent who patiently listens and dispenses wisdom, and as the trusted mentor who points us to Scripture when we are tempted to ignore it. We know His voice from reading and studying His Word, from paying attention to the Holy Spirit, and from spending time with Him in prayer. And when we find ourselves in situations where we feel frustrated that we cannot see Him, we can rest in the grace—the comfort—of recognizing His voice. For the time being, His face may be hidden, but His care, His will, and His way are ever available to us.

We can hear Him loud and clear.

READ JOHN 14:15–17.

1. Whose voice is the most familiar and distinctive to you? A parent's? A sibling's? A former teacher's?

2. Have you ever known someone who has a voice that is almost instantly comforting to you? Write about that a little bit.

3. Do you ever think about what God looks like? About what you would see if you were to meet Him face-to-face? Explain.

4. When is the voice of God clearest to you?

TODAY'S PRAYER

Day 43

*S*everal years ago there was a TV show about football that I loved. For the first two seasons, I was a loyal viewer, but a couple of years ago, the show changed its focus to a new school and a new coach. The drama was still compelling, no doubt, but over time my interest started to wane. And the more I thought about the reason for my changed attitude about a show I had enjoyed so much, the more I realized that the coach's relationships with his players were hard for me to watch. I'm all for a coach or leader being tough and getting the best they can out of the people in their charge, but what unsettled me was that this particular coach almost seemed to hold his players in contempt. His demeanor could be condescending and arrogant. As a result, he consistently seemed to be talking down to his players instead of coaching them up. Communication seemed mostly shaped by shame, not encouragement.

And let me tell you what: when I realized the dominant role of shame in the coach's tone, it was *super* convicting to me personally, and it has continued to challenge me, especially when it comes to sharing my faith with others.

Now to be clear: I understand that the football coach's job was to coach a football team, not share the love of Jesus. But watching the dynamics play out between him and his team was such a reminder of how important humility and sincerity are as we seek to love people well. We have to honor and esteem others, and their innate worth as image bearers of God must be at the forefront of our minds, especially when faith is the focus of the conversation. Why? Because as believers, we never want to go into a situation intending to love and minister to others but with an attitude of superiority or self-righteousness in our hearts. In fact, I think it's fair to say that self-righteousness has been an effective relationship builder approximately zero times.

So what does it look like to love and lead people like Jesus would? Here are a few things to think about:

1. **We love with great humility.** We are not trying to "win" or prove that we're right. We understand that Jesus is the point, we are not, and we deeply desire for others to see Him, not us. We get low by serving selflessly and sacrificially; we magnify the Most High God.

2. **We love with great intention.** We listen more than we talk. We pay attention to how people are hurting, we love them unconditionally, and we recognize that Jesus' ability to heal far exceeds our ability to "fix."

3. **We love with great confidence.** Jesus is our Lord and Savior. Why would we ever be afraid? We know He is the Source of everything good in our lives, so it is our great joy to share love, peace, and hope that can only and always come from Him.

The grace of God empowers us to love people right where they are—with no shame, no condescension, and no self-righteousness—just like God loves us. Share your faith today by loving like Him.

READ 1 JOHN 4:18–21.

1. Have you ever struggled with self-righteousness? With feeling some degree of moral or spiritual superiority? What's the danger of that?

2. How do you fight against a holier-than-thou attitude in your life? Are you able to recognize it if it starts to crop up in your thoughts or feelings?

3. Who is someone you'd like to love with great intention this week?

4. Who is someone who has loved you with great intention at some point in your life? What kind of difference did that make?

TODAY'S PRAYER

Day 44

Working with teenagers means that stories about choices and consequences are always floating around my office. From the everyday stuff (like an unintended but unkind comment to a friend) to the potentially life-altering stuff (like a pattern of deliberately defying authority), I often feel like I need to hang a sign on my office door that says Lessons Happen Here. And those lessons apply to me too.

I was thinking back on some of the stories and lessons I've witnessed in my office—family situations, personal heartaches, relationship struggles—and it occurred to me that when something really gets hold of us, it can feel overwhelming and even impossible to break free from it. That thing that gets hold of us might be co-dependence in our relationships; it might be deep, unsettling insecurity; it might be a pattern of keeping secrets and creating what feels like a double life. It could even be retreating into isolation because friendships just feel consistently disappointing and difficult. Regardless, here's what I've seen over and over again, in my own life and in my interactions with students: when something gets hold of us, we can start to feel really comfortable in that place, and moving into a healthier way of life—a place where there's some freedom—well, it is a FIGHT.

So how do we fight wisely? And how do we fight well?

1. **We get gut-level honest with God about what's going on.** Before we can begin to heal, we have to acknowledge our hurt, our sin, our anger—ALL OF IT—before the Lord. We need to know that we don't have to hide from Him, and few things are as liberating as honestly and candidly saying, "Okay, Lord, here's where I am." And if you know you need to ask His forgiveness, don't waste another second before you do. His unconditional love for you is real.

2. **We get gut-level honest with someone we trust about what's going on.** When we're emotionally or spiritually overwhelmed, our judgment can be pretty terrible. We need trusted, wise people

to help us navigate a path to freedom. That might be a parent, a mentor, a Bible study leader, or someone else. We don't need to be afraid of honesty and accountability—they're our friends.

3. **We get in our Bibles.** Here's the very best reason for this: we need Truth. Nothing tells us the Truth like Scripture: "For the word of God is living and effective and sharper than any double-edged sword, penetrating as far as the separation of soul and spirit, joints and marrow. It is able to judge the thoughts and intentions of the heart" (Hebrews 4:12).

4. **We get on our knees.** Prayer keeps us connected to the One who created us and knows us best. Consistent conversation with the Lord is critical because it reminds us that we don't have to hide from Him AND He is with us as we fight the good fight.

5. **We get connected to trusted, safe community.** Whether we're in a Bible study, a youth group, or a small group at church, we need to be in a place where we experience the love, the care, and the unconditional (truthful!) support of other believers. It's so good to learn to struggle out in the open and to have people who are committed to praying for you and with you. Healthy community is life changing.

Freedom can for sure be a fight, but the fight is worth it. Fight wisely. Fight well. The grace of God goes before you every step of the way.

READ 1 TIMOTHY 6:11–12.

1. Can you think of a time in your life when it felt like something bigger than you had a hold on you, and you weren't sure how to break free? Is anything like that going on right now?

2. Take some time to list the battles your friends and family members are facing right now, places where you know they're fighting for freedom.

_____

_____

_____

3. Read 1 John 2:1 and write it below.

_____

_____

_____

4. What does it mean to you to know that Jesus is your Advocate?

_____

_____

TODAY'S PRAYER

_____

_____

_____

_____

_____

_____

_____

_____

Day 45

*N*ow you may not have faced this particular challenge, but it's one that has surprised me with its frequency as I've talked with girls at school over the last several years. The issue is what I have come to think of as aspirational friendship, or when someone is only content in a friendship as long as it serves her purposes. Sure, a girl might enjoy the company of someone she hangs out with on the weekends, but she also constantly keeps an eye a little further up the ladder, always assessing and evaluating if she can slide into another relationship with a higher social status, always striving in some way to befriend a person she perceives as more popular.

This behavior is, of course, exhausting. And when you realize that a person you thought you could trust actually sees you as more of a stepping-stone than a sister, it's heartbreaking. It also ripples. Because feeling a sense of betrayal in a friendship, not to mention letting go of whatever expectations and security you associated with that friendship, can impact future friendships, especially if you don't take time to process and heal. It can make it hard to settle in and relax in new relationships when you can't shake the feeling that people will abandon you for someone they perceive as better or more relationally advantageous.

And don't miss this: maybe the hardest part about realizing that a "friend" was essentially playing a relational chess game is that you likely never saw it coming. So that's all a real carnival, right?

I've had countless conversations with girls who were reeling from friendship heartache, and while I always wish I had a nice, big bow I could use to tie up all the loose ends and make everything better, I don't. A disappointing end to a friendship is one of those things you can't walk around; you have to walk through it. And as you walk through it, there's only one thing of which I'm 100 percent confident:

> *Jesus will never leave you.*
> *Jesus will never leave you.*
> *Jesus will never leave you.*

I can't tell anyone what it will feel like to navigate such unexpectedly rocky territory. But I absolutely know Who will walk with you. I don't say that as a platitude or as hollow comfort; I say that because the Lord is faithful. I say that because He is the best, most trustworthy, most loyal Friend we will ever have. He cannot be disloyal or dismissive or unkind because those things are literally not parts of His character. He always listens, always comforts, and always cares. He is patient when we're frustrated, steady when we're weary, and wise when we're impulsive. You will not waste a single second confiding in Him, confessing to Him, and communicating with Him. He always—*always*—has your best interests at heart, and when you hurt, He is your very best Source for healing.

Jesus loves you just as you are and right where you are. When friendships go sideways, He holds. Rest in His grace and His peace today. He loves you so much.

READ PSALM 71:14–18.

1. Have you ever had your heart broken in a friendship? Think about this too: have you ever broken someone's heart?

2. How have hurtful or disappointing friendships in your past affected the friendships in your present?

3. When was the last time you talked really honestly with the Lord about the current state of your friendships? What parts of those relationships feel healthy and good? Where is there room for improvement or growth?

4. Do you think of Jesus as your Friend? Explain.

TODAY'S PRAYER

Day 46

No matter our age, it's hard to live in the moment. It's rare to feel truly settled and content in the here and now; we're much more likely to have our eyes set on some imagined destination down the road.

Last winter some recent graduates from the school where I work came by to visit. Based on what I knew from social media and from conversations with their moms, they had adjusted to their freshman year of college easily and beautifully. We had been talking for several minutes about all the excitement of their new phase of life when they surprised me by shifting the direction of our conversation. Suddenly they were reflective. Looking in the rearview mirror at high school, as it were, they began to list things they had taken for granted.

One girl said, "I miss being known the way I was in high school; most people at college still feel like strangers." Another girl said, "I miss adults other than my parents caring about me. I didn't realize how special it was to be genuinely loved by my teachers." For the next half hour or so, they continued to talk about what they had failed to appreciate even six months before, and as I sit here almost a year later, I'm still thinking about the significance of what they said.

Here's the deal: it's important to hope and dream about what's ahead. Anticipation is a wonderful thing. But it's also good, and so worthwhile, to recognize the everyday graces in our current season. We learn so much as we practice active gratitude, as we thank the Lord for what He is doing and how He is teaching us right here, right now, in the middle of what is probably a whole lot of ordinary.

Years ago an expression stuck with me: *Be where your feet are.* It's so tempting to live in the future, to try to predict what our lives will look like in two, five, even fifteen years, but the Lord has you where you are right this very minute for very good reasons. Today is a great time to (1) be where your feet are and (2) be grateful for the current state of your real-live life. That doesn't mean you're not facing some challenges—life is rarely easy, after all—but it does mean that you can take time to see how God is caring for you and providing for you in this particular season.

Think about your family, your school, your work, your church, your neighborhood, your city, your creative life, your passions, your home, your transportation, your meals, your friends, your music—all the pieces and parts of your day. And whether it's right here in this book or on a separate piece of paper, write down five (or more!) things you're really grateful for. Get specific about it. Although the next phase of your life will no doubt have its wonders, this phase does too. So don't miss them. Make gratitude a habit. It will serve you well and help you remember the Giver of all good gifts during every season of life.

READ ECCLESIASTES 3:1–8.

1. Do you think you make a habit of gratitude? Why or why not?

_____

_____

_____

_____

2. Is it easy for you to live in the moment? Do you dwell on the past? Or do you tend to focus on the future?

_____

_____

_____

_____

3. How would you rate this current phase of your life? Easy? Moderate? Difficult? Explain.

4. Does gratitude feel more natural to you when life is easy? Why do you think that is?

TODAY'S PRAYER

Day 47

*R*ight now I'm sitting at our kitchen table with an absolutely glorious view of a maple tree in our neighbors' backyard. Leah and Jeremy's tree looks like the very definition of "ablaze with color." The leaves are bright orange, almost neon in places, and every time I look up from my computer and catch a glimpse of them, I'm awed and grateful that God has made something so beautiful.

And that maple tree is making me think about something else.

The Lord uses lots of ways to plant good and beautiful things in the lives of our neighbors. Leah is an exceptional math teacher. My friend Joey designs and builds amazing theater sets. My friend Heather is a gifted high school administrator. My friend Joel is a brilliant radiologist. And as I sit here and contemplate the maple tree next door, it occurs to me that we can respond in different ways when we see a gift from God that doesn't necessarily belong to us:

1. **We can be dismissive of the gift.** Sometimes we feel threatened when someone has something we don't. For example, my friend Kasey is an incredible choir director. If I were living in a jealous or unhealthy place, I might think of reasons why her gifts are no big deal and maybe they're overrated. This isn't true, of course. Plus, this kind of reaction dismisses the careful, intentional work of God. If we see dismissiveness crop up in our reactions, we need to get to the root of that.

2. **We can wish the gift belonged to us.** If I were to sit here all afternoon and wish that Leah's maple tree actually lived in my backyard, you would probably tell me that was a dumb way to spend my time. You would be right. But so many times we can see our friends and neighbors use the gifts God has given them, and our response is to wish that gift belonged to us. I wish I could sing/dance/teach/paint/shoot three-pointers/run like so-and-so.

This response leaves us trapped in jealousy and focused on self. It's not our best look.

3. **We can delight at seeing God's gift in action.** This, my friends, is the ticket. When we see God entrust a gift to our friends and neighbors, our job is to cheer them on and thank the Giver. What joy to see my friend Melanie write a book that makes people laugh out loud! What grace to see my friend Conrad explain Scripture in a way that makes high schoolers want to know Jesus more! These things are not cause for apathy or jealousy; they are reasons to celebrate God's infinite kindness and creativity in the body of Christ. We can be so thankful!

Leah and Jeremy's maple tree has reminded me there is deep, inspiring grace in being able to appreciate the gifts God has planted in someone else's backyard, so to speak. Look for opportunities to affirm those good gifts today.

READ 1 CORINTHIANS 12:12-20.

1. When was the last time you were absolutely blown away by how the Lord has gifted someone? Who was the person, and what was the gift?

_____

_____

_____

2. What are some ways God has gifted your neighbors and friends? Try to list at least three people and their gifts.

_____

_____

_____

3. How do you respond when you see other people's gifts in action? Look at the three points in today's devotion. Do you respond more like 1, 2, or 3?

_____

_____

_____

4. Look up Hebrews 10:24. Write it out here.

_____

_____

_____

TODAY'S PRAYER

_____

_____

_____

_____

_____

_____

_____

_____

_____

_____

_____

Day 48

One of my favorite trails starts with a steep decline (you kind of have to jog down it to keep your balance) and ends with a steep incline (honestly, the sight of that hill intimidates me every single time). But the in-between parts, well, they feel a little bit like perfection. The trail is flat for just long enough, then hilly to get my heart rate going, then curvy in a way that keeps the view interesting. Some nice downhill sections give my calves a chance to stretch, and a couple of wide-open areas let the sun really show off. I have no idea who designed the trail, but I feel compelled to publicly affirm their choices and say, "KUDOS TO YOU, TRAIL DESIGN TEAM."

A couple of months ago I was walking the trail, delighting (once again) in the way it's laid out, and I realized that if I can feel such deep gratitude for a trail at a city park, how much more grateful should I be to my God for how He intentionally maps out our lives? For the countless ways He creates paths that lead us in the directions He wants us to go?

So here are a few things to think or pray about as we run (or, in my case, walk) the course set before us:

1. **Make sure you're prepared for the journey.** We wouldn't walk a rocky trail in high-heeled shoes. Traveling any path requires wise preparation. As we set out on the road the Lord has laid out for us, we need to be listening to trustworthy teachers and their good instruction. We need the Truth of Scripture along with the guidance of the Holy Spirit. We need constant communication with the One who made us and leads us.

2. **Watch where you're going.** Every trail has forks, shortcuts, and unexpected turns. Life is no different. Pay careful attention to the Lord to know where He wants you to go next. It's easy to blaze through turns without considering if those turns are taking you somewhere you had no intention of going. It's also easy to get tripped up if you're moving too fast. Slow and steady.

3. **Remember you don't have to travel alone.** Sometimes we buy into a mindset that life is ultimately a race where it's every person for themselves. Over and over in Scripture, however, we see how lives of service and ministry overlapped with other people's. Mary and Elizabeth. Ruth and Naomi. Paul and Timothy. Jesus and the disciples. Pay attention to the folks who are figuratively running alongside you. Those relationships might be some of the deepest and most rewarding of your life.

None of us are guaranteed an easy time as we travel. Most of us have run into obstacles that might remind us of that big hill at the end of the trail I love. But our lives are not random. The Lord plans and purposes our years on earth to build our character, to increase our faith, and to help us trust Him more and more. He puts us in positions where, no matter how hard the journey, we can grow in our desire to run our races well (Hebrews 12:1) and to give Him all honor and glory (Romans 11:36).

The Lord has designed your path with great intention. You were made for it!

READ PSALM 139:1—6.

1. Do you believe the Lord has designed your life with great purpose? Why or why not?

_____

_____

2. Do you think of yourself as a cautious person? Or more of a full-speed-ahead person? How does your personality affect the way you run your race, so to speak?

_____

_____

3. Has there ever been a time in your life when you felt like you wandered off course? Or maybe when you were determined to go your own way, regardless of how you sensed God was directing you? How did that work out? Did you learn any good lessons?

_____

_____

_____

4. How would you characterize this current phase of your life's path? Uphill? Downhill? Really steep? Particularly beautiful? Explain.

_____

_____

_____

TODAY'S PRAYER

_____

_____

_____

_____

_____

_____

_____

_____

Day 49

It's definitely not the wisest course of action, but sometimes when I'm initially confronted with something troublesome—particularly when it's something that might require medical care—my first reaction is denial. *If I ignore this, it is sure to go away. If I pretend like it's not bothering me, then maybe it will disappear.*

Yep. *Super* mature. *Super* wise.

If an issue persists for a few days, though, I typically cave and call my doctor. This is maybe the only area of my life where I think of fear as a friend, because it's not a sense of responsibility that drives me to seek medical help; it's pure, white-hot anxiety about what the worst-case scenario might be. In fact, I cannot count the number of times when I have sat in an examination room at my very kind doctor's office and informed him that I clearly have a dire, life-threatening illness. How do I know? Because Google told me so.

A few years ago I headed to the doctor because I was concerned about something that was likely a common skin condition but also possibly a symptom of a lethal strain of a brain-eating bacteria (this is how my mind works when I have unresolved medical issues). My doctor examined the problem, pronounced it nothing to worry about, and sent me on my way with a prescription for an antibiotic that would help everything get back to normal. And let me just tell you: when I walked out of his office not even thirty minutes after I arrived, I felt a profound sense of relief. It was as if I had walked in carrying fifty pounds of free weights and then floated out to my car like Mary Poppins holding a magical umbrella.

As I drove home, it dawned on me that it would be right and appropriate if I were to feel a similar sense of relief about the healing of my spiritual condition. Here's what I mean: as believers, we can get used to the gospel. We grow almost accustomed to the fact that Jesus took on every bit of our sin and shame when He was crucified; we can even get really casual about our relationship with our Savior who rose from the dead so that we might have eternal life. It's not that we're not grateful, but in ways both big and small, we can start to take the gift of salvation for granted. We forget that before we came to faith in Christ, we were dead in our sin. And even though we might not think about it very often, the reality is that we were doomed to live in darkness until the light of Jesus illuminated every part of our lives.

Having access to doctors who can treat our physical ailments is absolutely cause for gratitude and celebration. And let's also take time to be thankful for the joy that comes from knowing a Savior who heals our spiritual condition. Not only has He paid the penalty for our sin and secured our eternity in heaven, but He is also with us in the here and now, carefully tending to all the places we're broken, all the places we're hurt, and all the places we're sick. Even now He is patiently and carefully loving us back to life. What a Savior!

READ 1 CORINTHIANS 15:1–11.

1. Have you ever dealt with a medical situation that wasn't as bad as you feared? How did you respond to that?

2. Do you ever feel like you take the kindness of God for granted? Explain.

3. What are some specific ways that Jesus has healed you and changed you? How are you different now compared to before you knew Him?

_____

_____

_____

_____

4. Look up the lyrics to "Thank You, Lord" by Hillsong Worship (it's an oldie but a goodie). Write down the first verse here.

_____

_____

_____

_____

TODAY'S PRAYER

_____

_____

_____

_____

_____

_____

_____

_____

_____

_____

Day 50

A couple of days ago my friend Kasey recommended a documentary she thought I would like. It's about a dance studio that puts on a huge production for the community, and since the owner of the studio/head dance teacher is an actress I've admired and enjoyed watching for years, Kasey thought I would get a kick out of seeing her lead and coach in the context of preparing for a big event.

Oh. DID I EVER. And I didn't expect it, but I feel like I learned so much over those ninety-ish minutes. In fact, there's one lesson that I cannot shake, so I'm going to share it with you today.

There's a massive difference between perfectionism and excellence.

That's it. That's the lesson.

And the more I've thought about it today, the more I've been encouraged. Because here's the thing: we can all get caught up in perfectionism. We can get bogged down in thinking that we're defined by how perfectly we can do certain things, and we can get so discouraged when our inability to attain perfection reminds us of how very human we are. Somehow we've programmed ourselves to think we have to be the very best—the ultimate, even—at everything we undertake. Oh my goodness, that is an exhausting way to live. Perfectionism is so self-focused—so centered on how I do and what I achieve and how I perform—that there's no possible way it's healthy. It's also an impossible standard.

Why is it an impossible standard, you wonder? Because there is only One who is perfect. You and I aren't gonna make the cut, my friend.

But excellence? Oh, it is another story. And I also happen to believe that it's a *better* story . . . and one where we're much more likely to notice the real Hero.

Here's what I mean. In the show Kasey recommended, the dance teachers were constantly pushing their students, constantly encouraging them to be excellent. What I never heard a single person say, however, is that the dancers' performances had to be *perfect*. And I noticed that although the dancers moved with precision, they were not mirror images of each other. They moved with *freedom*. Every dancer was gifted, no doubt, and I don't know when I've witnessed more joyful movement on a stage. So there was a spirit of excellence, no doubt, but it seemed that the desire to be excellent was rooted in wanting to bless and entertain the audience, not in wanting to draw attention to self.

We may not realize it, but sometimes perfectionism is rooted in an unconscious desire to usurp God's glory. We want people to see us, recognize us, point us out as someone special. But excellence? Oh, it is a different deal. Excellence is when we make the most of the gifts we've been given, not so we can be recognized, but so our efforts bless others, honor others, and ultimately give glory to the only One who is perfect: Jesus.

Perfectionism will wear us out. Excellence, however, can become an offering and bless the people around us. Be excellent today in Jesus' name.

READ COLOSSIANS 3:23–24.

1. Do you think there's a difference between perfectionism and excellence? What is it?

_____

_____

_____

2. Have you ever dealt with feeling like you need to be perfect? What effect did that have on you?

_____

_____

_____

3. What are two or three areas of your life where you would like to consistently demonstrate excellence?

4. Are there believers in your life who consistently demonstrate excellence? Who? What do you notice about how they approach different tasks or responsibilities?

TODAY'S PRAYER

Day 51

I realize that this might make some of you say, "GET WITH THE TIMES, MAMAW," but I love Twitter. I do. I know it's not the newest or the fanciest of the social media platforms, but I don't care. I like the exchange of ideas. I like the 280-character limit. I like the fact that I've been a Twitter user since the year of our Lord 2007, which means I've been on Twitter longer than some of you have been alive.

I'm not gonna lie. That last thing is pretty humbling.

Nonetheless, I'm an avowed Twitter fan, even though people (tweeple?) (is that a step too far?) typically argue way too much and talk incessantly about politics and sometimes forget that they have an actual sense of humor. I tend to focus on the content that's uplifting or fun or encouraging, and that is why, for the most part, Twitter tends to brighten my day.

Yesterday was no exception. I scrolled through Twitter fairly early in the morning, and a tweet from my friend Rachel (@RachelAnneRidge in case you're wondering) stopped me in my tracks. I immediately wanted to share what she wrote with y'all.

Here's what she said: "Can you think of three individuals that you can bless, encourage, or help today? Write their names into your calendar or journal, then act on it. Be a difference-maker. Be a force of relentless grace."[2]

Isn't that the best? As believers we think a lot about God's grace, and rightly so. Grace is the completely undeserved love and mercy God the Father lavishes on us. It is forever and always a gift, and it touches our lives every single day. But what we may not think about as much are the ways *we* can extend that grace to others. We may not always consider what a game changer it is when the grace of God becomes an offering we share with the world. But, oh my goodness, it really does make a difference. And I absolutely love the idea of being *relentless* with grace. After all, isn't that what God does for us (Lamentations 3:22–23)?

---

2. Rachel Anne Ridge (@RachelAnneRidge), Twitter, February 5, 2021, 7:49 a.m., http:// twitter.com/RachelAnneRidge/status/1357687830202494979.

There are countless ways that you could be a force of relentless grace today, but just in case a list would be helpful, here are a few suggestions:

1. Say actual encouraging words to a friend on Snapchat instead of just sending a picture of your eyeball (y'all love some eyeball pictures).

2. Write a sincere note to a friend and leave it on her windshield.

3. Bake cookies for an elderly neighbor.

4. Pick up a friend's favorite coffee drink when you go through the drive-through—then deliver it with a homemade card.

5. Make a floral arrangement using greenery you find in your yard and a vase from underneath the kitchen sink—then share it with someone who needs some cheer.

6. Write some of your favorite Bible verses on index cards and hand them out to friends who need a little encouragement.

7. Make a playlist you know will be meaningful to a friend or loved one—and then text them the link!

Consider today how you might do exactly what Rachel suggested. Be a force of relentless grace in Jesus' name!

READ PHILIPPIANS 2:12–16.

1. Let's follow Rachel's lead: who are three people you could encourage today? Write down their names.

2. What are the specific ways you would like to encourage them?

_____

_____

_____

3. Who are the people in your life that have relentlessly extended grace to you? What has that meant to you? How has it encouraged you?

_____

_____

4. How is God's grace relentless? What are other words you might also use to describe His grace?

_____

_____

_____

TODAY'S PRAYER

_____

_____

_____

_____

_____

_____

_____

_____

Day 52

I can't read your mind, of course, but my guess is that wherever you live—an apartment, a house, a dorm room, wherever—something about that place drives you a little bit batty. Maybe it's a wall color that isn't your favorite, or a sink that doesn't drain like it should, or a chair that's a little worse for the wear after you accidentally baptized it with a big glass of fruit punch. For me it's the ivory-colored carpet in our hallway and bedrooms (by the way, WHO PUTS IVORY CARPET IN A HALLWAY?). The carpet was here when we bought the house, and over the years it's become increasingly difficult to keep clean. The edges always look super dingy to me, and since the carpet is such a light color, I feel like even spilled water leaves a stain.

So, just like you might cover that wall color you don't like with posters, or avoid using the stubborn sink, or drape the fruit-punch chair with a blanket, I have my very own coping strategy for the hallway carpet: inasmuch as I can help it, I don't turn on the hallway light. Sure, I know that the carpet isn't in pristine condition even when the light is off, but I like that the dark hides the evidence of what's really going on. Not to overdramatize a situation related to, you know, *carpet*, but most days it feels easier to ignore the situation than to turn on the light and feel frustrated by it.

And here's what every bit of this reminds me: sometimes there's stuff in our lives we'd rather not see.

Now, all things considered, our reluctance to take a long, hard look at carpet, furniture, walls, or whatever might not be that big of a deal. But where there are battles with sin—which might look like rebellion, secrecy, hatred, selfishness, or countless other ways we can grow comfortable in the darkness—we need to make sure we're being intentional about letting the light in.

Here are three ways we can do just that:

1. **Tell somebody.** So often when we struggle, we hide. We may even pretend like there's absolutely nothing wrong. But when we share the difficult parts of our lives with someone who loves the Lord and is trustworthy and wise, we choose light over darkness. This is such a good thing.

2. **Study Scripture.** Nothing illuminates our hearts and minds like the Word of God. No matter where you are in your relationship with the Lord—just getting started or walking with Him for years—committing to Bible study is an awesome decision.

3. **Pursue community.** We can absolutely access the light of Jesus Christ on our own through prayer, Scripture, and the Holy Spirit. Still, it's a beautiful thing to live openly and honestly in the company of other believers. Because sometimes the light that shines through Christians who know us and love us can show us the way.

There's no doubt that sometimes life feels dark. Thank the Lord today for all the ways He shines the light and helps us see.

READ JOHN 3:19–21.

1. Is there something in your home that really bugs you so you do your best not to see it? Write about that a little bit.

2. Is there something in your head or your heart that you're content to leave in the dark? Write about that too.

3. Why do you think secrecy—or hiding—can feel so comfortable at times? Why do we fall into believing that it's a perfectly reasonable way to live?

4. What's one area of your life that needs the light of Christ today? Explain.

TODAY'S PRAYER

Day 53

*O*ne day last week I cranked the engine of my car, and within seconds it was Alerts Aplenty on my dashboard. All four of my tires were low on air, and I knew I needed to add air as soon as possible. So later that afternoon, when my husband and I left the house to run some errands, I said, "Hey, let's run by the gas station and put some air in my tires." Behold responsibility!

When David started to fill up my tires, I learned something. I guess I had never really paid attention, but when each tire reached the prescribed level of fullness, my horn honked. At first, I thought the honking horn was some weird glitch, but by tire number three, I realized, *Ohhhhh, that's the signal that the tire is full.* And then, a few minutes later: *It would be so great if a similar system helped me measure the fullness of the Holy Spirit in my heart.*

Here's what I mean by that: sometimes, no matter how good our intentions might be, we struggle to be people who demonstrate the love and peace and joy of Jesus each day. We're more motivated by what we want than what Jesus would want, and whether it's the result of our impatience, our self-centeredness, our stubbornness, our rebellion, or a combination of all the above, we assess the condition of our hearts and notice Alerts Aplenty. Something is off. But unlike the situation with my tires, we can't run to the gas station and solve the problem.

We're not helpless, however, and praise the Lord for that! There are so many ways that we can increase our dependence on the Holy Spirit. We can confess our struggles to the Lord. We can talk with trusted friends and mentors. We can pray. We can worship. We can listen to sound teachers. We can replace any lies we've come to believe with the Truth. We can read our Bibles and participate in Bible study. In fact, I recently saw a tweet from Scott Sauls, a pastor in Nashville, and he said this: "A sure sign we have been filled with the Holy Spirit is a new affection and thirst for Scripture."[3]

---

3. Scott Sauls (@scottsauls), Twitter, December 19, 2020, 11:47 a.m., https://twitter.com/scottsauls/status/1340352955950788608.

Granted, all these things will be *slightly* more time-consuming than putting air in our tires, and you won't actually hear a horn honk when you're sufficiently filled, but you will likely notice a change in what you're thinking about, what you desire, how you're treating people, and how you manage the demands of your days. This is all such a good reminder of how gracious the Lord is to us. He knows that we are, as "Come Thou Fount of Every Blessing" says, "prone to wander," but He doesn't cut us off or shut us down when we get off course. He not only paved the roads of confession, repentance, forgiveness, and restoration, but He also faithfully keeps them open and available to us.

Whether we're running low on faith or running a little too high on ourselves, here is what remains dependable and true: grace upon grace will make a way. Thank You, Lord.

READ JOHN 6:60–65.

1. Can you remember a time when you felt like you were running low spiritually? When was that?

_____

_____

_____

_____

_____

2. What were some of the warning signals that indicated you weren't in a great place in your relationship with the Lord?

_____

_____

_____

_____

3. Did you initially pay attention to those warning signals? Or did you try to ignore them?

4. What happens to a car when we ignore the warning lights? Is there a good lesson there for humans as well?

TODAY'S PRAYER

Day 54

Several months ago I was asked to fill in for our school's sweet librarian for a few days. So on a bright Monday morning, I walked across the building for my first day of library duty. I was full of optimism. However, within about ten minutes, I'll have you know I was officially overwhelmed.

Junior high students wanted to check out books, but I had no idea where anything was. High school students wanted to borrow iPad chargers and send documents to the printer, but I wasn't super confident about how to do either of those things. By lunchtime I felt completely discombobulated; I didn't know how to check in books on the computer, I had neglected to keep up with the book-requests spreadsheet, and I was utterly clueless about how to find book three in the *Percy Jackson* series, among countless others. If my morning was any indication, I had signed up for the longest week of my life.

On Tuesday, though, I started to find my way. There was actually a folder with all sorts of instructions in a drawer of the circulation desk, but I had been too overwhelmed to pay attention the day before. After I read through the folder, I logged into the computer, I practiced scanning books in and out, and I took some time to commit different sections of the library to memory: biography was here, mysteries were over there, science fiction was under the big window. By Wednesday, I felt like I had gained some library skills, and by Friday, I was enjoying myself so much that I wondered if I could stay in the library another week. Granted, it would take me years to know and understand everything our librarian does on a daily basis, but I was happy to have enough basic knowledge that I didn't frustrate the students who just wanted to read a book.

As I have looked back on my week as a wannabe librarian, I've realized that (1) it was so much fun doing something new and different, and (2) I was *super* hard on myself during those first couple of days when I was trying to steer around a significant learning curve. I like to think I'm patient with the new cashier at the grocery store or the server in training at a favorite restaurant. But with myself? Not so much.

When I was an English teacher, I would see this same behavior with my students. They would get so discouraged the first few days we were learning something new—like how to document sources or analyze a poem. But after they practiced and realized they were making progress, they would settle in and enjoy themselves. For some reason we want to be certified as Awesome and Instantly Exceptional at everything we do, but we have to give ourselves the necessary grace and time to learn new things. After all, Scripture tells us "do not despise these small beginnings" (Zechariah 4:10 NLT), so when a new opportunity to work or serve presents itself, we need to remember we weren't born experts. Our responsibility is to patiently pursue whatever the Lord might be leading us to discover. When we feel unqualified or ill-equipped, we can trust Him more and more. He is our Hope!

READ HEBREWS 4:14–16.

1. On a scale of 1 to 10 (with 10 being extremely patient and borderline angelic), how patient are you when you're learning something new? Are you more patient with other people than you are with yourself?

2. When was the last time you felt challenged or frustrated by trying to learn something new? How did you respond?

3. Why do you think fear often runs beneath the surface when we're trying to learn or do something new? Why are we afraid?

4. Can you think of a time when something new turned out to be a "small beginning"? Maybe you took a dance class, felt totally intimidated, and then ended up sticking with it and loving it? Or maybe you joined a small group at church and then experienced amazing relational and spiritual growth? Write about that a little bit.

TODAY'S PRAYER

Day 55

*O*ne of the topics I think about more than any other is leadership. Maybe it's because I've worked with students for so many years, but I love to identify leadership in people, I love to evaluate what makes leadership effective, and I especially love to encourage leadership when I see it in action. I'm one of those people who believes that if you see something good happening, NAME IT. So I have no doubt caught a few people off guard when I've walked up to them after a choir performance or football game or chapel service and said, "You led like crazy while you were performing/playing/speaking." And here's why I make a point to do that: some of the most natural leaders have no idea that they're leading. They don't realize what an impact they have on the people around them.

If you had asked me about leadership when I was younger, you would have gotten a vastly different take on what constitutes a leader than what I would say now. Back then I would have said that leaders were people with power, people who got their way, people who were able to control large groups and push their agenda through. Leaders were the folks I viewed as large and in charge, so to speak, and I thought very little about their character, their motives, or their methods.

But now? Oh my goodness. I know beyond a shadow of a doubt that character, motives, and methods are essential to humble, servant-hearted, God-honoring leadership. A leader esteems, values, honors, and cares for people. A leader calls people to be better and reach higher. A leader builds up others, serves selflessly, operates without ego, and lives with integrity. A leader inspires trust. And a leader tells the truth.

There's not a doubt in my mind that there is an area of your life where the Lord has gifted you to lead. Maybe it's in the place where you work, maybe it's in a preschool Sunday School class, maybe it's with younger siblings, maybe it's on the volleyball court, maybe it's on the math team—I could go on and on. But here's the important part: whenever and wherever you find yourself in a unique position to inspire, encourage, and, as a friend of mine says, "make the room you're in a better place," do not lose sight of the fact that true leadership gets low. It serves. Real, impactful leadership prefers helping and lifting up others over glorifying self. That's why it's such a difference maker.

It's tempting, of course, to seek glory for ourselves, to prioritize power and control over loving people well. But don't miss this: self-focused, self-serving leadership is poison, and it contaminates everything it touches. As people who profess Jesus as our Savior, we lead differently because He has shown us how to lead from love: selflessly, sacrificially, boldly, enthusiastically, and freely. Your leadership won't just make someone's day better or make the task at hand easier. Your leadership can be a tangible, visible extension of the grace, mercy, compassion, and love of our heavenly Father. The places where you realize you have the opportunity to love and serve others are not accidental. You are there on purpose. For God's purposes. Get low and lead.

READ 2 CORINTHIANS 8:7–9.

1. In what areas of life do you feel you have the opportunity to lead?

2. What kind of leader tends to get your attention? Someone who is action-oriented? Someone who leads by example? Someone who is consistently faithful in doing small things well? Explain that a little bit.

3. Who are a couple of people you really admire in Scripture? Why?

_____

_____

_____

4. Name two or three specific people in your life who model humble, compassionate leadership. What do you admire about them?

_____

_____

_____

TODAY'S PRAYER

_____

_____

_____

_____

_____

_____

_____

_____

_____

_____

_____

_____

_____

Day 56

$\mathcal{J}$'ve said it before, and I'll say it again: if I could, I would blow up the phrase "friend group" with a stick of dynamite. Because do you know how many conversations I've had about friend groups over the last six or seven years in particular? INFINITY CONVERSATIONS. And yes, that is a totally legitimate number.

It stinks, but the amount of heartache that has been caused by friend groups—particularly among the high school girls I work with—well, it is significant. People think they're in a certain friend group but are then shut out of it. People want to be in a certain friend group but feel like they're not allowed access. People wonder if they'll ever find their friend group. People don't like their friend group anymore but don't know how to leave it. People wonder if their friend group is too dramatic or too clique-y or too gossip-y.

(Maybe you can understand why I've grown a little weary of the phrase "friend group.")

Despite my frustrations with the terminology, though, I totally get the frustrations behind the phrase. We are people who are made for relationships—made to know and to be known. So when those core desires are threatened, dismissed, or complicated in some way, fear roars like a lion. *What if we never find our people? What if people never find us? What if we start to feel like we're trapped with people we don't actually like all that much?*

In light of the stress of a current or future "friend group" fiasco, here are a few things to remind yourself or someone you love who is navigating rough relational waters:

1. **Deep friendship takes time.** As eager as you may be to find your forever friends, there will likely be some bumps along the way. Know that the Lord is increasing your empathy and your compassion even when friendship feels hard. He is teaching you

what you do and do not need in relationships. These are good, redemptive lessons that come out of difficult situations.

2. **Commit to being the kind of friend you'd like to have.** My friend Melanie says this all the time. If we want friends who are honest, trustworthy, loyal, and kind, then we need to practice being people who are honest, trustworthy, loyal, and kind. We have to let the Lord shape our hearts and character.

3. **Lean on Jesus.** To be clear, I'm not saying you need a "Jesus is my friend group" T-shirt (OR AM I?), but a healthy, growing relationship with the Lord has a way of putting our relational frustrations into perspective. He is steady. He is true. He loves you. And He will always be your safe place during difficult times.

Having a great group of friends can be wonderful, no doubt. But finding friends can also be stressful. And no matter where you are today on that spectrum of friendship, know that the Lord is there with you. His grace, compassion, and kindness are constant even when friends are fickle. He will never leave your side.

READ PSALM 36:5—9.

1. Have you ever had your heart broken in a friendship? Write about that a little bit.

2. How do you feel when you hear the phrase "friend group"? Happy? Eye roll-y? A little exhausted? Like you also would like to blow it up with a stick of dynamite?

3. Do you feel pressure—internal or external—to have an established, easily identifiable friend group?

4. Why do you think there can be resistance to the notion of being friends with everyone instead of belonging to a certain group? Why is there such a tendency to name our friends and put them on lockdown, so to speak?

TODAY'S PRAYER

Day 57

$\mathcal{I}$'m convinced most of us have had an area of ongoing struggle in our lives. In most cases we're not powerless against that struggle, but we might need to fight it more often than we'd like. Whether we're dealing with addiction, depression, anger, bitterness, or a myriad of other issues, we can get so tired of fighting—and decide life would be easier if we gave up and let that struggle have its way with us.

That's not true, of course. Logically we know that when our behaviors are destructive, we're harming ourselves and likely causing the people who love us to suffer as well (when you care about someone, it's hard to see them in pain). And more often than not, we want to get better or do better or feel better, but we're just not sure how. We feel overwhelmed by the process in front of us. We don't want to fail—maybe even fail *again*—and feel that disappointment. We forget that God's mercies are available to us every single day, in every single struggle.

I understand this brand of spiritual amnesia. For as long as I can remember, I have battled my weight. And listen, I have fought it in some dumb ways. When I was younger, I was a sucker for a fad diet. When I got older, I was a sucker for some good, old-fashioned denial. And about ten years ago, I decided I was tired of fighting, so I gave up. I stopped trying altogether.

Five years into giving up on my health, I was in the worst shape of my life. I was tired. Everything made me winded. No matter where I went, I calculated how far I might be required to walk, and one day, after I climbed approximately ten steps and could not catch my breath, I wondered if an actual heart attack might be in my future. I was beyond discouraged. It was like a five-year free fall, and then, I literally fell and broke my foot. I spent two months in an orthopedic boot. And in the middle of all of that, my mama died. It didn't exactly feel like a season of my life that was filled with hope.

Later that summer, my orthopedist told me that I needed to walk on a treadmill to strengthen the muscles in and around my foot. Since I was tired of the boot, I took his advice. I started walking, very slowly, and within the first week I was so encouraged by how much better I felt that I wondered if I could keep going. I knew the Lord, in His mercy, had made a way for me to start exercising without feeling embarrassed about being so out of shape. And day after day, I grew increasingly motivated to keep walking and moving in the direction of better health.

Five years later, I'm still walking. Not every single day—but most days. Even though I'm nobody's "after" picture, I'm much healthier. I'm committed to moving in the direction of victory instead of worrying if I'll be able to escape defeat. This is such a relief: knowing that the Lord's mercies are new every morning, knowing that if I mess up, I don't have to sit in shame, knowing that He can make a way when it feels like there is none.

No matter what your struggle is, our gracious God has made a way for you today. Your job is to stand up and walk in it. Just today. New mercies will meet you tomorrow.

READ LAMENTATIONS 3:21–24.

1. What are one or two persistent struggles in your life?

2. Do you ever feel ashamed or embarrassed that you have to fight those particular battles? What do you do with those feelings? Do you talk about them?

3. What would it look like for you to move in the direction of victory? What is a forward step you can take, just for today?

4. What does verse 22 in Lamentations 3 remind us about the Lord's mercies? Why is this truth significant for us in our struggles?

TODAY'S PRAYER

Day 58

*O*ne of my favorite things about Scripture is how the Lord can teach us so many lessons from a single passage. We might read a few verses on, say, a Monday, and conclude our reading with two or three clear takeaways; then we can go back to that same passage a week or month or year later and notice something totally different. It's an experience that never fails to encourage me, mostly because it's such a reminder of the depth of the truth of Scripture. We will never get to the bottom of it.

One recent aha moment with a familiar passage happened when I was reading in Exodus 17 about the Israelites fighting the Amalekites. While Joshua stayed on the ground with the troops, Moses went to the top of a nearby hill and raised his staff on the Israelites' behalf. As long as he held up the staff, the Israelites would do well, but when his tired arms lowered the staff, the Amalekites would prevail. Clearly Moses wanted the Israelites to win the battle, but it was understandable that his arms would grow weary. So Moses' brother Aaron and a man named Hur moved a rock so that Moses could sit down, and they held up his arms. Sure enough, the Israelites were victorious.

THOSE GUYS, right?

With a battle raging all around them, Aaron and Hur offered support that was *visible* and *clear*. No one had to wonder where they stood or what side they were on. No one had to guess if they were committed to the Israelites' cause in general and Moses' responsibilities in particular. They stood visibly and clearly with Moses, visibly and clearly with the Israelites, and visibly and clearly with God.

Over the course of your life, you will have countless opportunities to figure out where you stand on a controversial issue, a prolonged battle, or an ongoing injustice—and then decide the best way you can offer your support. Of course it's encouraging to whisper "you can do it" behind the scenes, but it could well be a game changer for people in your community to receive help in the great wide open. You might wonder why it's a big deal to openly stand with a friend who's struggling, or to participate in an important cause that's near and dear to a family member, or to volunteer your time to an issue connected to your faith. But the encouragement of your involvement will ripple in ways you may not know or see. You can't even imagine how your visible, clear support might impact people who have been in the thick of the fight for a long time, people who are eager for victory or resolution or an end to the battle.

You likely won't mimic the exact actions of Aaron and Hur and literally hold up someone's arms. But over the course of your life, you'll have countless opportunities to figuratively lift the arms of the folks in your life, to help them fight the good fight, to encourage them to keep going. And your visible, clear support will also speak volumes—*I see you. I am for you. I am here to help.*—to people you may not even know are watching.

Remember, *the Israelites weren't fighting for power; they were fighting for deliverance.* As we obediently respond to the places and people where the Lord prompts us to offer visible, clear support, may the same be true of us.

READ EXODUS 17:8–13.

1. Can you think of any places where you have recently considered offering your support? A non-profit? A cause or an issue? A particular person you've wanted to help? Make a list here.

2. What might it look like to support those organizations or individuals in a way that's visible and clear?

3. In general, what holds you back from getting involved or speaking out when you encounter a cause or issue that matters to you?

4. What's the difference between fighting for power and fighting for deliverance? Explain.

TODAY'S PRAYER

Day 59

$\mathcal{I}$ want to talk to you today about revenge.

Yep. I get it. Probably not the topic you were expecting.

Nonetheless, we see revenge all around us, right? In movies, for example, we watch characters devote their lives to payback, to making sure the person who harmed them personally or hurt their family or betrayed their friendship pays for what they did. And in real life, we hear people talk about how they're going to teach their old boss a lesson, or they're going to make sure so-and-so experiences pain for what they've done, or they're going to ruin someone's life if it's the last thing they do.

To be clear, this is a whole different deal than justice, which is man's attempt to make wrong things right. Revenge doesn't make anything right; it just trades wrong for wrong. And that's why we have to remember that Jesus is on the side of justice. He is never on the side of revenge.

Because I work with teenagers (who are human, after all), I do sometimes deal with kids hurting other kids; it's one of my least favorite parts of the job. Sometimes the hurting is deliberate, sometimes it's not, but the fallout can be heartbreaking. And listen—we could spend the rest of this book chronicling all the mean things we've seen people do to one another; but in school life, a lot of the meanness happens on social media, on group texts, and through the power of the rumor mill. Some of the most awkward conversations of my life have been because someone just made up something and then spread the lie like it was a full-time job. And when you're sitting in the heartache of someone doing that to you—of someone deliberately setting out to hurt you—well, revenge can feel a little bit like justice.

Don't fall for it, though. Revenge is not justice. Revenge will not fix it. Revenge will not make the situation better.

Instead, seek wisdom. Genuine, God-honoring wisdom. Use the channels available to you to pursue justice, absolutely, but remember that you won't fix a broken situation by setting it on fire. And here's the thing about wisdom that's rooted in the knowledge and grace of God: it will always lead you in the direction of peace. Ideally you will have peace and reconciliation with the person who hurt you, but if for some reason that isn't possible (for example, if the person isn't sorrowful or repentant about what they did), you will have peace because your conscience will be clear.

Revenge is the path to regret. Listen to the Lord and to the wise voices in your life, and instead pursue the path of wisdom and peace. God's grace will lead you there, and God's grace will hold you as you heal.

READ JAMES 3:16–18.

1. Why is wisdom so critical when you're processing feelings of hurt or betrayal?

2. Why can revenge seem like a better outcome than justice? (It's not, of course—just asking why it can seem that way.)

3. Can you think of a time when you have been tempted to seek revenge? Write about that a little bit.

_____

_____

_____

4. Look up Romans 12:18. Write/doodle/illustrate it here.

_____

_____

_____

_____

TODAY'S PRAYER .

_____

_____

_____

_____

_____

_____

_____

_____

_____

Day 60

I can't remember a time when people have been more divided about, well, *everything*. Think of a topic, and there's a vocal group *for* that thing, a vocal group *against* that thing, and group of people who feel caught in the middle. The division plays out on social media, in the workplace, in our churches, and around dinner tables, and both the tone and frequency of the disagreements are exhausting. We're divided on issues of justice, theology, education, history, medicine, and politics, just to name a few. And since so many people are yelling, there's not a lot of bridge-building. You've probably seen the polarization in your community or even in your family. Oh, it's all a real carnival, except the rides aren't working, the funnel cakes are spoiled, and there's a twisted, scary vibe happening with the clowns.

Now, nobody has asked me to examine or solve this cultural phenomenon where everybody seems to feel immensely frustrated with each other, but it has occurred to me more than once that in people's efforts to be right, we may have forgotten what it means to be compassionate. To empathize. To really, deeply listen—not so we can refute an argument, but so we can try to understand the other side.

God has created every single person with inherent honor and dignity. He has created every single person in His image. So when our friends and neighbors are fighting for change in a certain area because they're hurting, or they have suffered in the wake of ongoing injustice, or they're straight-up convicted that something isn't right, we need to pay attention to what they're saying—*especially* when we struggle to understand their viewpoint. Why? Because we're commanded to love our neighbors (Mark 12:31). Because Scripture tells us to weep with those who weep (Romans 12:15). Because we mourn with those who mourn.

And don't miss this: if we find that we're too angry or bitter to weep with those who weep, then we need to dig in and get to the bottom of that. Dismissing or diminishing someone else's pain is the opposite of how Jesus repeatedly responded in Scripture. He leaned in, He listened, and He comforted. He told people the truth for sure—and He called out sin when He saw it—but as I wrote in *Stand All the Way Up*, there was no bragging, no insulting, no demeaning, no belittling, no shaming, no manipulating, no deflecting, no side-stepping, no power-grabbing, and no fearmongering.

In His own deeply divided time on earth, Jesus *honored* people. So if we need encouragement to love our neighbors well during these difficult days, we only need to look at how Jesus lived and loved: the listening, the healing, the truth telling, the parable-ing (totally a word), the challenging, the serving, the feeding, the cautioning, the calming, and the blessing. I think we can agree these are far better options than the yelling.

Yes, times are hard, and times are tense. But as believers we want to make every effort to bring the peace and grace of God into hard conversations as we try to understand each other. We want to love our neighbors well. And we can do these things with confidence, because as we listen with our hearts as well as our ears, we trust that Jesus can bridge our gaps.

READ ROMANS 12:14–18.

1. What issue or conflict in the world feels especially tense to you right now?

_____

_____

_____

_____

2. Do you have a strong opinion about that particular issue? What is it?

_____

_____

_____

3. As you think about people on the other side, how do you feel? Are you angry? Confused? Concerned?

_____

_____

_____

4. Why is it important to try to understand people with whom we disagree? How can we love them well as we do that?

_____

_____

_____

_____

TODAY'S PRAYER

_____

_____

_____

_____

_____

_____

_____

_____

_____

_____

Day 61

*T*his weekend I went to lunch with a friend. She happens to be brilliant and hilarious and insightful—just a delight of a human being—and she loves the Lord like crazy. In fact, most of our conversation centered on our faith: what we've been learning, how we've been struggling, what questions we're asking, and how looking to Jesus in all of these things is changing us.

I left our lunch encouraged and grateful. Friendships marked by sincerity and compassion are a treasure, and as I drove home, I thought about how feeling understood brings such rest and comfort to our hearts and minds. If it's possible for lunch on a heated patio to bring peace to your soul, then ours certainly did. So I couldn't help but laugh when a completely different thought occurred to me.

The world might say we're competitors.

It sounds strange, but it's true. This friend of mine also works in podcasting—she co-hosts a very successful podcast, in fact—and there's some overlap between our audiences (just so you know, though: her podcast has many, many more listeners). Now, to be clear, we most certainly are not competitors, but since we are two people who do similar work in the same field, people might assume we're somehow locked in a tense, ongoing competition for downloads, social media follows, speaking engagements, etc. I don't know why we assume people who have similar interests/skills/jobs must secretly wish for each other to fail, because that is usually not the story.

The reality is that my friend, who is one of the best analytic, strategic thinkers I know, is always happy to help when I have questions about the business side of podcasting (which, admittedly, is NOT MY STRONG SUIT). She constantly cheers on my podcast partner, Melanie, and me. She invites us to participate in fun, podcast-y things, and she genuinely roots for our success. I think she would say that Melanie and I have done the same (although we probably don't do as many fun, podcast-y things, but you understand what I mean). The bottom line is we don't see her and her podcast partner as competitors; they are our *friends*, and man, is it ever our joy to encourage all the great things they're doing.

So often we're inundated with messages—both subtle and overt—about winning at all costs, looking out for number one, and prioritizing our own success. These messages are garbage. When God has entrusted people with good, uplifting gifts, then the best-case scenario is for those gifts to be shared with as many people as possible. That means we encourage, we spur on, and we rejoice in what God has done and what He will do as our friends share their talents. This isn't because we want them to be famous or make a bunch of money or go viral online; it's because we want our friends to bless others as they share their talents, and we want God to get every bit of the glory and honor He is due.

We will likely regret the times we let competition sneak into a relationship as a result of our fear, jealousy, or self-doubt. However, we will likely *never* regret the times we sincerely encourage and affirm our brothers and sisters in Christ. They have such good gifts to share with the world. Celebrate what God is doing in their lives!

READ HEBREWS 10:23-25.

1. Have you ever felt like you were in competition with a friend because you shared similar gifts or interests? Write about that a little bit.

_____

_____

_____

2. Do you sometimes feel threatened by the gifts or talents you see in your friends?

_____

_____

_____

3. Why is jealousy such a destructive force in our relationships? Is jealousy a battle for you right now? Explain.

4. How could you celebrate a friend's gifts today? How could you be an encourager?

TODAY'S PRAYER

Day 62

One of my favorite all-time books is *To Kill a Mockingbird* by Harper Lee. In chapter three, there's a line—something the father, Atticus, says to his daughter, Scout—that I think about all the time: "You never really understand a person until you consider things from his point of view . . . until you climb into his skin and walk around in it."[4] Scout doesn't realize it, but Atticus is teaching her a lesson in empathy, which just so happens to be an invaluable quality when it comes to loving our neighbors. Empathy isn't just the recognition that someone is hurting or sad or happy or grieving; empathy is feeling those things with the other person because we're acquainted with those emotions too. Empathy is loving someone from a place of *understanding* as opposed to merely *acknowledging*; it is truly compassionate comfort. In fact, it's the kind of comfort that Jesus offers us.

Living an empathetic life seems like it would be easy enough, but it's often more difficult than we realize. There are all sorts of reasons why, but here are three of the biggest ones:

1. **We're inherently self-focused.** As sinners, we are prone to think about ourselves and our problems and our needs before we prioritize others.

2. **We sometimes scroll through things more than we sit in the reality of things.** We can doomscroll on our phones for three straight hours without really feeling anything. Heartache becomes information more than it becomes an invitation to lovingly respond.

3. **We're numb.** It feels like the world blows up every fourteen minutes. Our own lives can be overwhelming, and emotionally, we're maxed out. So it may seem easier to dismiss the realities of someone else's situation than to try to understand and empathize.

---

4. Harper Lee, *To Kill a Mockingbird* (New York: Grand Central Publishing, 1960), 39.

Before we write off the need for empathy, though, let's consider this:

1. **Part of loving our neighbors well involves actively caring and praying for them in difficult times.** When we're close to someone, we demonstrate our empathy by looking out for them, checking on them, and listening to them. And regardless of how close we are, we can *pray* from a place of empathy, with a sincere desire for mercy and peace and comfort to cover them.

2. **When someone tells you something is hard for them, believe them.** Even if you can't understand it yet, believe them. If your temptation is to minimize or even to criticize the fact that someone is struggling, resist that. Lean in. Pray. Empathize.

3. **We reflect the heart of Jesus when we sincerely, compassionately, and empathetically care for one another.** Jesus was never so busy or self-focused that He missed opportunities to minister. When He encountered people who were hurting or struggling in some way, He stopped. He very literally heard their cries for help, and He *cared*. In His power, we can do the same.

Let's resist the urge to look past other people's heartache; instead, like Atticus said, let's "consider things from [their] point of view." The empathetic concern and compassion of a friend can be the grace of God in challenging times. Let's lean in, listen, and love empathetically.

READ JOHN 11:32–35.

1. Who are a few people you know who are genuinely empathetic? How does their sincere concern affect other people?

2. Is it easy for you to feel empathetic? Or does it somehow feel safer to keep your distance emotionally? Why do you think that is?

3. How do you think Jesus' empathy in today's Scripture reading impacted the people around Him? What assurance does it offer us now?

4. What's one way you could express empathy to a friend or loved one today? What's one way you could let someone know that you don't just see their hurt, you're feeling it with them?

TODAY'S PRAYER

Day 63

$\mathcal{I}$ grew up in a church where we heard about grace a lot. It was an ever-present theme in our Sunday sermons, and the message of grace was consistent and strong. I knew from a young age that Jesus loved me unconditionally, that He died for all sinners sacrificially, and that He would forgive me endlessly. So when I put my hope in Jesus and trusted Him for salvation, I knew I would never have to pay the penalty for my sin. The fact that I didn't deserve any of this was nothing but the grace of God. And since He is incapable of breaking His promise of salvation—since there is nothing I can do to make Him take it back—I have been well aware that His grace is what holds me, sustains me, and carries me every single day of my life.

As long as I've had some degree of understanding about God's grace, I've been grateful for it. Awed by it, even. But when I was young and immature in my faith, I viewed God's grace as a Get Out of Jail Free card. If I knowingly made a bad choice, no big deal because God would always forgive me. If I said something really unkind, no big deal because God would still love me. If I acted in ways that didn't reflect God's character, just relax, everybody, because God would have my back.

This was all true, of course. It still is. But what I didn't understand (and listen, I have spent so much time in my adult life trying to figure out how I missed this part) is that the grace of God shouldn't be a way for me to justify making bad choices because *Yay! Forgiveness!* Instead, the grace of God is what enables me to identify and contemplate my bottomless capacity for selfishness, to understand that there is absolutely no sin beyond my reach, and to recognize my helpless spiritual state apart from Him. The grace of God is not my license to do whatever I want; instead, God's grace upon grace is the only reason why I would ever desire to turn from sin and grow in holiness. In fact, that grace—and the unmerited abundance of it—is precisely what enables us to change in ways that reflect the heart of our heavenly Father.

I've heard many Bible teachers say that when we use grace as an excuse to continue in sin, that's *cheap grace*. So when we count on grace to cover the intentional indulgence of our sinful impulses, we treat it as transactional, almost (*I'll do this, God, and then You can give me more grace and forgive me*). Call it situational amnesia, or call it pride, but we forget that grace is an "indescribable gift" (2 Corinthians 9:15).

The reality is that the undeserved grace of God came at an enormous price. We can only know this grace because of the "Lamb of God who takes on the sins of the world" (John 1:29), because Jesus exchanged His righteousness for our unrighteousness (2 Corinthians 5:21) so that all who believe in Him will have eternal life (John 3:16).

If you find yourself tempted to justify your habitual or deliberate sin today, remember this: while God's grace does guarantee we'll be spared the eternal consequences of our sin, we cheapen His grace when we use it as justification for making bad decisions. The grace of God compels us to turn from sin and pursue holiness. This grace is anything but cheap. It's priceless.

READ ROMANS 6:1–4.

1. What does it mean to you, as a believer, to be a recipient of God's grace? Is it easy for you to believe God loves you that much? Or do you struggle, to some degree, to believe it?

2. Can you think of a time when you have used God's grace as an excuse to continue in sin? Or to do something you knew was unwise?

3. Are there areas of sin or disobedience in your life where you feel prideful? Where it seems easier to hide behind cheap grace than to confess and ask the Lord to help you change?

4. What are two or three areas of your life where you would love, by God's grace, to walk in growing holiness?

TODAY'S PRAYER

Day 64

*I*f there has been a recurring narrative in my conversations with high school girls over the last seven years, it's this: *I feel like I have to be perfect in all the ways. I need to make incredible grades. I need to excel at sports. I need to be charming and kind and beautiful. There's no room for me to mess up, slow down, or take a break. I feel like I am running a race that never, ever ends, and I'm not enjoying it.*

These feelings aren't exclusive to teenagers, by the way; women of all ages feel these same pressures. Somewhere along the way many of us have internalized the lie that our primary aim in life is to be awesome at everything while making it look effortless, all the while being a delightful, winsome person who loves the Lord and never misses an early morning quiet time.

No biggie, right? Easy as pie. And I guess because I've had so many conversations with this recurring theme, I feel really sensitive to the ways women live with the burden of these pressures. I don't believe women put these expectations on themselves as the result of any one malicious voice; instead, it seems like it's a combination of things that become collectively overwhelming: family, school, health, work, social media, with a dose of self-imposed shame to top it all off.

Last weekend I was shopping for a few things for our house when I ran across an assortment of decorative signs. There were the usual suspects: "Gather," "Live Laugh Love," "Thankful," etc. But there was one that stood out. It was at the end of the aisle, displayed above a sign with a Walt Disney quote, and it said this: "Happy girls are the prettiest girls." I'm not proud of it, but my instant reaction was white-hot anger. In fact, I wanted to punch that sign in the throat. Apparently I wasn't the only one, because when I posted about it online later that day, a like-minded commenter responded, "KILL IT WITH FIRE."

Her response made me laugh because my initial reaction was likely a little, um, *strong*, but there are so many frustrating messages out there about who women in general and young women in particular need to be.

And heaven forbid that you feel like you have to manipulate your emotions (be happy!) to meet the world's standard of pretty. THAT'S A HARD NO. Because what Jesus offers us is freedom from every bit of those burdensome expectations. Jesus offers us abundant life (John 10:10), not an endless list of rules and tasks that exhaust us. He is far less interested in how we look and behave than He is with the condition of our hearts. And while yes, living and working in the places where He leads us will always bring challenges, our identities don't rise and fall on our achievements. Our identities are secure in Him; we just want to be fruitful and faithful with whatever He entrusts to us.

So today? Stop. Breathe. Rest. Your worth doesn't depend on your mood or your performance. Your value doesn't depend on perfection. How do I know? Because Scripture makes it clear. You are fearfully and wonderfully made (Psalm 139:14), you are fully accepted by Jesus (Romans 15:7), and you are free (John 8:36).

READ MICAH 6:6–8.

1. As a general rule, do you put a lot of pressure on yourself?

_____

_____

_____

_____

2. What tends to be your greatest motivator? Achievement? Other people's reactions? Feeling like you did your best? Something else?

_____

_____

_____

_____

3. Is there an expectation—whether it's self-imposed or coming from someone else—that's weighing you down right now? Is there a way to manage that expectation in a healthier way?

4. Do you ever fake a certain mood to try to manage what people think about you or how they react to you? How does that make you feel after the fact?

TODAY'S PRAYER

Day 65

I realized something pretty significant about myself when I was in junior high school: my personality changed depending on where I was. I had one personality at home, another at school, another at church, another if I was with an older group of friends—you get the idea. Even though I had very little interest in examining the reason for it at the time, it nagged at my conscience, and I knew it was a part of myself I didn't necessarily like.

I wonder if you have ever felt the same way. On one hand it's not terrible to be able to "read a room" and dial up (or dial down) your personality accordingly (nobody wants to have a pep rally at a funeral, for example). But it's a whole different deal when you're consistently disingenuous/fake/trying way too hard to be someone you're not. When you act differently to gain people's approval, the situation can get pretty dicey relationally. Eventually, whether we like it or not, people will get tired of wondering which version of us is going to show up.

I wish I could tell you my junior high personality challenges worked themselves out by the time I got to college, but NOPE. It took a really long time for me to feel like I was the same person no matter what. Part of that was dealing with some of my own insecurity; part of that was learning to be vulnerable instead of sarcastic (sarcasm was my superpower in my early twenties); and part of that was realizing it was important to me to be the same person no matter what.

But here was the biggest aha moment of all: in every situation where my personality changed, I was worried primarily about other people's opinions of me. I was trying to be the person I thought they expected me to be, and here's why that was a bad idea: it would have been far better for me to go into situations wondering how I could love and serve people instead of putting myself at the center of every interaction.

If you think about it, Jesus never tried to win over the crowd. We don't see any instances in Scripture where He was trying to be the most hilarious or the most clever or the most intelligent person in the room. He loved people, He told the truth, and He cared for people deeply. I mean,

I'm sure He was a delightful person—what with being the Savior of the world and all—but He was always, ALWAYS others-centered.

It took me a long time to realize that my ever-changing personality was rooted in a whole lot of selfishness (and I believe I've already mentioned the insecurity, thank you very much). But that understanding helped me shift from trying to manage other people's reactions to focusing on how I could better love and care for others through the power of the Holy Spirit. In fact, any time I'm about to meet a new group of people, here's what I pray: "Lord, give me great affection for these people. You made them, and You love them. Help me to love them too."

Ask the Lord to give you new people to love today, and trust the Holy Spirit to help you do it.

READ GALATIANS 1:10.

1. Is it difficult for you to have the same personality in every situation? Why or why not?

_____

_____

_____

_____

2. Have you ever been in a situation where you realized you were acting like a completely different person? Or, at the very least, you didn't feel like you were acting sincerely? Explain that a little bit.

_____

_____

_____

_____

3. Look up John 3:30. Write/illustrate/doodle it here.

_____

_____

_____

_____

4. If you could change anything about the way you interact with new groups of people—especially in terms of representing Jesus—what would it be? Explain.

_____

_____

_____

TODAY'S PRAYER

_____

_____

_____

_____

_____

_____

_____

_____

_____

_____

_____

Day 66

One of my very best friends, Melanie, also happens to be a gifted, hilarious, thoughtful author. Several years ago she wrote her fourth book, *Church of the Small Things*, and it's all about how God is at work in the ordinary, everyday parts of life. So often we spend our days waiting for the next big thing in our lives, but Melanie reminds us of all the ways we see God's faithfulness in the small stuff: an energizing walk outside, a meaningful conversation with a friend, or a walk-off home run in the bottom of the ninth inning. (That was my list, not Melanie's. I hope she approves.)

I think about Melanie's book all the time, mainly because I'm convinced she's right. While big moments can be great, everyday joys are the things that make a meaningful life. In fact, in chapter 12 of Romans—which happens to be one of my favorite books of the Bible— the apostle Paul chronicles some of the small, everyday things we can do to live and love effectively as believers. There's not a single instruction to build something big or maximize our influence. Instead, Romans 12 reminds us to "share with the saints in their needs; pursue hospitality" (v. 13). We don't have to make a habit of grand gestures; instead, Paul is telling us to live with a heart posture of seeing a need, meeting a need, and welcoming others.

I saw the sweetest evidence of how small things make a big difference just a few days ago. It's been an enormously stressful time in our country (I don't have room to get into the specifics, but for about 322 different reasons, Americans have been on edge), and we're all feeling extra dependent on members of our military and intelligence communities to keep us safe. The night before last I was flipping channels on the television when I saw live footage of one of our nation's leaders talking with members of the military. At first I couldn't make out what he was saying, but then I heard him loud and clear: "What's your name, sir? How long have you served?"

And that is when I burst into tears.

I can't presume to know how that National Guard member was feeling, but I know he was far away from home, and I know he was serving in a precarious security situation. So to see a high-level national leader make the time to go from person to person and show compassion—to offer a tiny bit of hospitality in an unfamiliar city—it felt like a small thing that might make an enormous difference in someone's day. In someone's life, even. There have been so many stories of dehumanization in the news lately, so many instances of people being dismissed and discredited for this or that reason, so many examples of people being really unkind to one another, so bearing witness to a sincere act of kindness (small as it was) felt like great big hope in the middle of a whole bunch of heartache.

As you go through your day, consider how the ministry and the power of small things might help you better love your neighbor, who might well be a stranger. Lord willing, you'll meet their small need in a big way.

READ ROMANS 12:9–11.

1. Can you think of a time this past week when small things have made a difference in your day? Explain.

_____

_____

_____

2. List the names of three or four people you would like to encourage this week, not with a grand gesture but with something small and meaningful.

_____

_____

3. As you read today's passage from Romans, what parts of Paul's encouragement most resonated with you? What feels like a way you'd like to love your neighbors with greater intention?

4. Look up Romans 12:21. Write/illustrate/doodle it here.

TODAY'S PRAYER

Day 67

As I write this, our son is a junior in high school with just three semesters left until he graduates. I'm not totally sure how that's possible since he was seven years old just a few weeks ago, but here we are. Fortunately, since I work at his school, I get to see him in that environment every day, and while initially I don't think either of us knew what to expect from being on the same campus, it has been the biggest blast. Part of the reason it has been so fun is because while I really love Alex a lot (as you can imagine), I love being around his friends. For the last four and a half years, I've had the privilege of spending an inordinate amount of time with them, the girls in particular. And one of the neatest things about that has been seeing how the Lord is working in their hearts, minds, and relationships as they get older.

Their maturity is especially evident in their friendships with each other. When the girls in Alex's class were in seventh grade, a group of fifteen to twenty girls would come to my office for lunch a few times a week. I remember their wide-eyed expressions as they would file in with braces, big smiles, oversized sweatshirts, pastel-colored pants (pastel denim was all the rage back then), fleece-lined boots, and a serious assortment of floral lunch bags. Usually at least one of them was on the verge of tears, and while the girls really did love one another, they sometimes struggled with practicing discernment in their conversations.

Here's what I mean: as the girls listened to each other, they sometimes didn't take time to think about what might be going on beneath the surface of someone's comment, and they didn't always pay attention to the unintended consequences of their responses. Lunch could feel like a not-at-all-enjoyable festival of misread and misunderstood conversational cues. Someone might say something that indicated she was dealing with some self-doubt or even shame, and people would react with remarks that sounded harsh or insensitive, even though that wasn't the intent. This would lead to hurt feelings and misunderstandings and occasionally even arguments.

Several weeks ago some of those same girls—now juniors—were in my office for lunch, and I realized how carefully and compassionately they were talking and listening to each other. The girls were practicing so much wisdom and discernment, in fact, that tears sprung to my eyes. It was such evidence of the Lord's faithfulness, of the girls' ever-increasing sensitivity to the Holy Spirit, and it was encouraging, to say the least. Even when someone perceived there was more to a story—or maybe some lingering heartache behind false bravado—she didn't wield her discernment like a bat over her friend. Instead there was a genuine willingness to love one another by prioritizing people's feelings over a desire to tell them what they needed to do or should have said. The girls heard what their friends were saying—and what they weren't saying as well. There was relational safety in that room. And I'll have you know that I didn't have to help settle a single argument when lunch was over. I promise I'm smiling.

The grace of God enables us to do better when we know better. Let's ask the Lord to help us be discerning and loving in our conversations today; let's ask Him to help us be safe, compassionate listeners for our friends and loved ones.

READ 2 CORINTHIANS 1:12–14.

1. What helps you to feel safe, loved, and heard in conversations? What shuts you down or makes you defensive?

_____

_____

_____

2. Who do you know who is a really good listener, someone who hears what you're saying and what you're not saying at the same time?

_____

_____

3. Have you ever felt like someone was listening to you to gather information instead of trying to understand? Explain that a little bit.

4. When it comes to conversations with friends, are you more wise and discerning now than you were five years ago? What are some things the Lord has taught you?

TODAY'S PRAYER

Day 68

I mean this as no offense to the dentists of the world, but I can't stand going to the dentist. I imagine that the whole experience would be much more pleasant and enjoyable if it didn't involve an assortment of people prodding and scraping and drilling inside my mouth. So it's hard for me to prioritize making an appointment where I'm going to experience some significant discomfort. I'd much rather do something, you know, *fun*.

For the longest time my personal dental philosophy was to pretend that everything was okay until it wasn't. This meant that I would skip checkup after checkup until I had a toothache that wouldn't quit, or it hurt to chew on my right side, or I broke a tooth while eating a potato (this actually happened). But even in the wake of a clear dental crisis, there would still be some stretch of time—maybe a few days, maybe a few weeks—when I would try to ignore the problem and wonder if it would just fix itself. Then, when hope ran out and I actually went to the dentist, I felt embarrassed for him to see the shape my teeth were in. I felt some degree of shame and failure because my negligence had led to the problem. Surely my dentist resented my need for help, right?

Thanks to the care of a really compassionate dentist, I realized after many years that—get ready for this—my dentist didn't go into dentistry so he could treat a bunch of people who had never had a cavity. In fact, he anticipated he would have to treat people like me, people with fears or hang-ups or just plain stubbornness when it comes to dentist-y things. His goal is never to lay down harsh judgment or impart shame or let a patient sit in their misery. He doesn't expect his patients to be perfect dental specimens; he meets us where we are because he wants to make us better. He is a dentist because he wants to help people who need it. And the more I've been able to recognize all of these things, the less I procrastinate when it comes to scheduling regular checkups and taking care of problems quickly.

It's interesting, because I have witnessed the same pattern in my relationship with Jesus. I put off dealing with something that really needs attention, and then I start to assume that Jesus wants me to fix it before I ask Him to get involved. I assume He will be absolutely disgusted that I didn't handle the situation perfectly from the get-go, and by the time I begrudgingly talk to Him about the thing, I feel embarrassed and ashamed.

Here's the undeserved grace upon grace of God, though: just like my dentist didn't go to dental school to serve people who don't actually need his help, Jesus didn't come to save sinless, shined-up people. He is a come-as-you-are Savior, and whatever our needs happen to be, He is always willing to not just comfort us in our pain, but to examine us, treat us, and heal us. Through the power of Scripture and the Holy Spirit alive within us, He can always show us the root of the problem. The more we trust His care (and make no mistake, His care is always trustworthy), the more we'll check in with Him on a regular basis instead of waiting until we're in a spiritual emergency.

By His grace, Jesus is always available to us, even when we've tried to put off dealing with a difficult situation. Praise the Lord—He is a Savior for sinners!

READ MARK 2:13–17.

1. What's something you tend to put off longer than you should? A checkup? An overwhelming assignment? A difficult conversation?

2. Have you ever felt embarrassed about your need for a doctor, a counselor, a dentist, or some other kind of healthcare professional? Why do you think we can sometimes feel almost guilty when we have to admit that we're not well?

3. Have you ever felt embarrassed about something you've confessed to Jesus? Explain that a little bit.

_____

_____

_____

4. Read Romans 10:11. Write/illustrate/doodle it here.

_____

_____

_____

TODAY'S PRAYER

_____

_____

_____

_____

_____

_____

_____

_____

_____

_____

_____

_____

_____

Day 69

*W*hen it comes to decorating our house for Christmas, I give myself a solid C on the grading scale. Don't get me wrong, I love Christmas, but I don't love having to set up and then pack up a bunch of decorations. So I always put up a Christmas tree (somebody give me a medal!), I always decorate said tree, and I always adorn the buffet area in our living room like it's a mantel (our fireplace doesn't have a mantel because, well, I don't even know why). But as far as stringing outdoor lights and finding places for lots of treasured Christmas mementos around the house, I'm a no. Planning and executing all of that stresses me out. Apparently I need a Low-Key Decorative Christmas to keep the mood merry and bright.

My friend Stephanie, on the other hand, TURNS IT OUT with the Christmas decorations. She puts up five beautifully decorated Christmas trees. The inside of her house feels like the most elegant winter wonderland you have ever visited. There are decorative pillows and cozy throw blankets, there are gorgeous accent pieces that evoke the wonder of the season, and there are garlands and ribbon at every turn. Not to mention that her outdoor Christmas lights are *on point.*

So if I get a C in decorative Christmas cheer, Steph gets an A+. Her holiday house looks absolutely gorgeous. And really, the thing that makes those decorations so inspiring and so meaningful is the sincerity behind them. Steph delights in the season. Her love for celebrating the birth of her Savior, well, *that's* what makes all of us want to sit in her house for hours on end. Her house doesn't just look the part; it's a genuine reflection of the condition of her heart.

I've thought about this a lot lately when it comes to Christians interacting with people who don't share our faith. It can be tempting to adorn ourselves with all the stuff that makes us look like a representative of Jesus: church attendance, online posts about our quiet time (I'm grinning), a Bible with our name embossed on it, a cross necklace, or a T-shirt from our most recent weekend retreat. But if people don't see sincerity behind all that stuff, or if, heaven forbid, the way we treat people is consistently unloving or condescending, our profession of faith won't translate to a hurting world. If our witness is couched in pretense, it won't be long-term effective. It may not even be believable. Maybe that's why Romans 12:9 says, "Don't just pretend to love others. Really love them" (NLT).

As Christians, we certainly don't want to dress up the external parts of our lives if the internal parts—our hearts, souls, and minds—don't bear witness to the transforming love of Jesus. Carrying the latest Christian bestseller (or the latest journaling devotional, amirite?) may feel like a great way to signal to the world, *Hey, I love the Lord*, but what's even more effective is when we back up the book we're carrying or the shirt we're wearing with humble, sincere, loving actions. When we don't pretend to love but actually love. When our lives are marked by the grace, mercy, and joy that can only come from Jesus.

Today is a great day for your sincere love of Jesus—and people—to shine through!

READ JOSHUA 24:14–15.

1. Can you think of a time when you've tried to "look the part," whether that's as a Christian or as something else? Explain that a little bit.

2. Have you ever been hurt because someone wasn't who they appeared to be? If so, how did you handle that?

3. What do you think sincere faith looks like? If you were to identify seven or eight crucial characteristics of sincere faith, what would they be?

_____

_____

_____

4. Can you think of a few people whose sincere faith is a source of encouragement for you?

_____

_____

_____

TODAY'S PRAYER

_____

_____

_____

_____

_____

_____

_____

_____

_____

_____

Day 70

I don't mean to brag, but I can be quite the fortune teller when I set my mind to it. Oh, I'm not saying that my predictions are *accurate* or anything like that, but on certain days—when I'm operating out of just the right mixture of fear, anxiety, and a deep desire to control—I can get waaaaaaay down the road in terms of how a certain situation might work out. The next thing you know, an imagined (IMAGINED!) disagreement with a family member has irretrievably broken our relationship and left us with no other option than to go on a nationally broadcast talk show where we publicly air every bit of our relational dirty laundry and share all of our hurt feelings. There are, most certainly, tears.

As you can tell, this is a totally logical scenario.

But the what-ifs in our lives—they can be so tempting, can't they? I mean, if something bad is going to happen, won't it be at least a little bit easier if we've taken some time to anticipate it? After all, there are so many what-if possibilities:

- What if I don't get into the college I want?

- What if my best friends abandon me?

- What if I can't figure out what to do with my life?

- What if I *think* I've figured out what to do with my life, and then I hate it?

- What if I have to move far away from my family?

- What if I have to stay in this place forever?

- What if I never fall in love?

- What if I fall in love, but the other person isn't in love with me?

- What if I move somewhere and have a hard time making friends and feel very lonely and my only dependable companion is Hulu?

A couple of months ago I had a conversation with one of our junior girls at school, and her anxiety about the future was so dialed up that she had a what-if question for just about every comment I made.

"You would be a great high school principal," I said. "WHAT IF I REALIZE I DON'T LIKE TEENAGERS?" she responded.

"You don't have to figure everything out right now," I said. "WHAT IF I DON'T FIGURE IT OUT, AND THEN I DON'T GO TO THE RIGHT COLLEGE, AND THEN MY LIFE IS RUINED?" she responded.

"The Lord is going to make every bit of this clear to you," I said. "WHAT IF HE DOESN'T LET ME KNOW IN TIME?" she responded.

We laughed about our conversation a few days later. But listen, I totally get where she was coming from. There are so many possibilities ahead, and trying to make the very best decisions can feel overwhelming. So here's what I want to remind you (and me) today: the Lord has a plan for your life. Not a single second of your life catches Him by surprise. Remember Isaiah 41:13: "For I am the LORD your God, who holds your right hand, who says to you, 'Do not fear, I will help you.'"

You don't have to worry, and you don't have to panic. He's with you every step of the way.

READ ACTS 20:22–24.

1. What is your biggest area of worry right now? Why do you think it feels like such a big deal?

_____

_____

_____

_____

2. Do you get bogged down in what-ifs? And if you do, what do you think prompts it? Is it fear? A desire to be in control?

3. What are three things you know to be true, no matter what? Three things that no what-if can touch?

4. Look up the hymn "All the Way My Savior Leads Me." Write out the first verse here.

TODAY'S PRAYER

Day 11

*T*his will probably come as a shock to you, but dating relationships—particularly in high school—can be a little, um, *dramatic*.

Some of you just laughed out loud.

And this isn't the case for everyone, of course. It is, however, the case for lots of people. Just getting to the point where you want to go out with someone can feel like an intricate, endless maze, and sometimes it takes the work of roughly seven to nine people to arrange a three-hour date. Add to that the actual challenges and responsibilities of a dating relationship, and there's a significant number of opportunities for misunderstandings and hurt feelings and broken (or, at the very least, *sprained*) hearts.

When it's a healthy relationship, though, that makes all the difference. Sure, there may be challenges, but a healthy relationship brings lots of opportunities to grow in faith and trust and love. A healthy relationship can be deeply instructive; in fact, it can help you understand what's important to you, what you need from another person, and where your expectations get out of whack. And even if a healthy dating relationship comes to a natural end, it hopefully brings some perspective and wisdom that will be helpful moving forward. These are great lessons.

Over the years I've had lots of conversations with girls about their dating relationships, and for the most part I try to remain cautiously optimistic and encouraging. Where I will get all the way fired up, though, and where I struggle to stay quiet (to be clear, I usually don't stay quiet) is when a girl feels like she has to settle for being someone's secret. There is no open interest demonstrated at school, church, work, or wherever; there are no get-to-know-you trips to Starbucks; there are no awkward asks on a date. There are, however, plenty of snaps, DMs, hey-do-you-want-to-hang-outs, and maybe-we-can-meet-up-laters. This kind of relationship is confusing as all get out, because there are no clear expectations, no clear boundaries (Are you dating? Are there other girls still in the picture? Is this going anywhere?), and no accountability to the people who love you and look out for you. After all, if the majority of a relationship is happening in secret, then there's no one bearing witness to it.

And you, my friend, are no one's secret. You deserve to be loved in the light.

It is completely understandable to be flattered by someone's interest or attention—to feel like you've been singled out—but it's good to remember that nothing grows in the dark. You are worthy of being cared for out in the open, and you don't have to settle for someone who, for whatever reason, doesn't understand that or flat-out can't handle it.

You are deeply and completely treasured by your heavenly Father (Daniel 10:19). You are a child of the light (1 Thessalonians 5:5). You have the mind of Christ (1 Corinthians 2:16). You were never meant to be someone's secret, my sister. Don't let anyone convince you otherwise.

READ EPHESIANS 5:6–10.

1. What are your healthiest relationships? I'm not necessarily talking about dating relationships, just relationships where you know you are valued and safe. What makes those relationships feel healthy?

2. When you think about a dating relationship, what qualities strike you as being most important, or even essential, to keeping things healthy?

3. Is shared faith foundational to a healthy dating relationship? Explain that a little bit.

_____

_____

_____

4. Have you been in a dating relationship that ended badly? What impact did that have on you?

_____

_____

_____

TODAY'S PRAYER

_____

_____

_____

_____

_____

_____

_____

_____

_____

_____

_____

_____

_____

Day 72

This past summer and into the early fall, I did a lot of my trail walking late in the afternoon. The weather was cooler, which was a real plus, and it was also a great way to process and shake off whatever stress I'd been carrying throughout the day. During those late afternoon walks, I got accustomed to the way the light filtered through the treetops, and when I got to the part of the trail with a clearing, I especially loved how the light almost looked like it blossomed in the open space. The sun didn't shine so much as it glistened, and after a long day, I couldn't help but exhale as I took in the beauty all around me. It was stunning, really.

Walking in the afternoons got trickier as we moved into fall. The days got shorter, this book you're reading demanded more of my attention, and a bout with COVID-19 kept me off the trail for a few weeks. I finally made my triumphant return (that's strong language, to be sure, but I was obnoxiously happy to see the trail again) on a Saturday morning in December, and it was the sweetest reunion. I wasn't quite in Snow White mode—there was not, in fact, any talking to birds—but in my head, at least, I marveled at *everything* (*Look at the pine straw! Look how the leaves have fallen! Look at the branches!*). And then, when I got to the crest of the second hill, I stopped dead in my tracks.

The light looked completely different.

The sun was shining on a different part of the trail, and since there were no leaves to filter it, the light seemed harsh, more direct. I studied it for several seconds before I realized it was enabling me to see things I had never noticed: a stream at the bottom of a drop-off, the profile of a distant building off to my right, and twenty trees so bent that they must have been on the receiving end of a violent gust of wind. I thought about what I'd seen as I eased down the hill, and an idea dropped into my heart so loudly that it almost echoed: *sometimes the light hits different.*

It was true that day in the woods, and the more I thought about it, the more I realized how much it also applies to our faith. Sometimes the light illuminates our deep gratitude for our families. Sometimes it clearly shows us our sin. Sometimes it makes us notice a person we've overlooked or a behavior we've tried to justify for way too long. Sometimes it helps us to see the Truth of Scripture with more clarity. But whenever the Lord shines a spotlight on the dark or unseen places in our hearts and moves in with His all-consuming, life-changing light, it is merciful. It is kind. And it should remind us that He is faithful.

Just like the sunlight on the trail, the direction of God's light can change with the seasons of our lives. We may be surprised by what it reveals, but no matter how the light hits, it is grace upon grace—and the Source is always the same.

READ JOHN 1:1–9.

1. Can you remember the last time you had an aha moment about something? When you realized you were suddenly seeing a situation or place or person differently? Explain that.

_____

_____

_____

_____

2. What are some ways you make sure light is shining into your life? Truth-telling friends? Journaling? Scripture? Worship? Write about that a little bit.

_____

_____

_____

_____

_____

3. Why does darkness sometimes seem more appealing than light?

_____

_____

_____

_____

4. Look up James 1:17. Write/illustrate/doodle it here.

_____

_____

_____

_____

TODAY'S PRAYER

_____

_____

_____

_____

_____

_____

_____

_____

_____

_____

Day 73

So I know we normally save the questions for the end of each day's devotional, but today I want to ask you to answer a couple of questions at the beginning, because they will frame our time together.

If you had to identify five of your strengths, what would they be? I'm talking about things like "loyal," "fair," "intelligent," etc. Write those in the column on the left. Then, on the right, list five characteristics that you would consider weaknesses. If I were listing weaknesses for me, for example, I might say, "procrastinator" (it's true), "stubborn" (also true), "impatient" (I AM SO BAD AT PATIENCE), etc.

1.   1.

2.   2.

3.   3.

4.   4.

5.   5.

So often we pay a lot of attention to our strengths. And listen—it's good to know your strengths because (1) you're awesome and (2) it's great to be able to identify the areas where the Lord has gifted and equipped you. It's also good to remember not to take those things for granted because you can help a lot of people by putting those gifts to use. I will also say that if one of your strengths is being detail oriented, I would like to request that you lend me just a tiny part of your brain, thank you so much.

And even though you might not feel this way, it is actually *fantastic* to be able to identify your weaknesses. Not so you can disqualify yourself and feel bad about yourself and wish you were different. NOT AT ALL. It's because if you love the Lord and are living for Him, you are going to be blown away by how He changes you in those areas. That doesn't mean you won't continue to struggle, but it does mean you won't be stuck in the same degree of struggle forever. He *will* change you.

Here's an example: I mentioned that I sometimes like to procrastinate. I put things off. When I was younger, that procrastination made me super irresponsible—like, gold medal-level irresponsible—but now I understand that procrastination takes a huge toll on me, especially spiritually and emotionally. So while I can still procrastinate in smaller ways—doing the laundry, picking up the dry cleaning, taking a package to the post office—the Lord has taught me so much about how truly destructive procrastination can be in my life. Yes, it's a weakness, but when I think about it, I'm so grateful for how the Lord has helped me in that area. I mean, the fact that I actually *finish* books after I start writing them is proof of the Lord's faithfulness and power.

Your strengths are your rock-star areas. You will naturally serve so beautifully in those places. But don't discount the gift of your weaknesses. That is where you will see the Lord do so much good work—where He will teach you, humble you, change you, and strengthen you over and over again. He truly will do what you cannot—what you can't even imagine is possible (Ephesians 3:20). His power at work in you is the grace of God.

READ GALATIANS 2:20–21.

1. Do you give the Lord credit for your strengths? Write a couple of sentences and thank Him for entrusting you with good gifts!

_____

_____

_____

_____

_____

2. Do you give yourself a hard time about your weaknesses? Have you ever thanked the Lord for them? Have you ever considered that He has entrusted you with weaknesses too?

3. Which one of your weaknesses annoys you the most? Do you feel like you fight it all the time? Or have you just decided that's how it will always be?

4. What is one specific way that a particular weakness affects your day-to-day life? How does it get in your way, so to speak?

TODAY'S PRAYER

Day 74

$\mathcal{T}$here have been times when I have found myself in a conversation where, for some reason, I could not seem to shut my mouth. Usually I have done this when I get hit with nerves or anxiety in the middle of a tense conversation, but instead of saying, "You know what? I need to get my thoughts together. Let's find another time to talk," I just start to overshare and fill every silence with even more words and eventually reach the point where I wondered if I was making any sense at all.

When I started working with the girls at my school, I had to ask the Lord to help me with how I handled conversations. I didn't want girls running out of my office and into the hall screaming, *"SHE WOULDN'T STOP TALKING."* It only took a couple of weeks for me to realize that I had a habit of jumping into deep conversational waters without asking the Lord to direct our words and help us listen with our ears as well as our hearts. I learned that a simple prayer before a hard conversation could be transformational at bringing peace and calm into a tense or anxious situation. It has been such a good lesson.

I also learned how helpful it is to intentionally reflect on a conversation after the fact. This is not always a strength of mine, but if we want to be loving listeners who show Christlike compassion when we talk to people, these questions can be invaluable:

1. **Were my words necessary (Proverbs 29:20)?** Did I dominate the conversation? Did the other person get to say everything they needed to say? Did I interrupt?

2. **Were my words helpful (Ephesians 4:29)?** Did I diminish or dismiss what the other person needed to talk about? Was I empathetic? Was I encouraging? Was I comforting? Did I explain myself clearly? Did I speak out of love or out of anger?

3. **Were my words true (Proverbs 8:6–8)?** Was I honest? Was I sincere? Did I give false hope? Did I point the other person to Jesus?

Asking these questions may seem unnecessary, but I cannot tell you how many times I've gone back to someone to apologize when I've gotten one (or more than one) of these things wrong. I've also gone back to someone and said, "Hey, I neglected to tell you something I should have." Sure, most of my hard conversations are when girls come to me for advice or to settle a conflict with a friend, but taking time to reflect after a long talk has also been really helpful for me in my conversations with my own friends.

Whether you've struggled with Conversational Regret or not, it's good to remember that prayer and reflection are wise ways to grow in grace as we talk and listen to each other. Let's ask the Lord to help us care for others really well by saying things that are necessary, helpful, and true in our conversations today.

READ PSALM 141:1–3.

1. Do you go to people for advice very often? Do people come to you for advice? Or is it a combination of the two?

_____

_____

_____

_____

2. Are you more comfortable giving advice or taking advice? Why do you think that is?

_____

_____

_____

_____

3. How do you normally respond in conversations that are tense or maybe even uncomfortable? Do you go radio silent? Do you talk too much? Something else? Explain that a little.

4. Do you remember the last difficult conversation you had? Reflect on it with the three questions in the devotional. Can you learn anything from it?

TODAY'S PRAYER

Day 75

$\mathcal{L}$et's just say you're a junior in college with a full class schedule this semester. You're also working a part-time job and lining up an internship for next fall. You're involved in several organizations on campus (résumé building for the win), and you're leading a Bible study for junior high girls at church. You're dating a cute guy who loves the Lord—and you think there might be a future there—so you're trying to be wise and intentional about spending time with him. Plus, you room with some dear friends, and it's good for your heart to hang out with them. But this week you have two papers to write, a huge test to take, and a group project to finish even though three of your group members have bailed. Also, you haven't talked to your little sister in weeks, your parents keep asking when you're coming home, and you have about 154 unread emails and texts.

If you're looking at the big picture, not a single one of these things is bad. You're super fortunate to be in college, to have great relationships, and to be in a spot where you can really prepare for the future. You have a family who loves you, and even though school can feel like a lot, you know you can push through—even if you don't get to sleep as much as you'd like. Sure, the (hypothetical) week is intense, but it's not impossible.

On the ground level, though, staring all this stuff in the face feels overwhelming. And even if you're not actually a junior in college right now, you can no doubt relate to a scenario where you look at your week and feel like you're being asked to eat an elephant. It's just so much, right? And because you're conscientious and driven, you're not just figuring out how to get by; you're trying to figure out how to eat that elephant *with excellence.*

This kind of pressure is precisely why you might kick off your week by sitting in your car with tears streaming down your face because All The Stress is making you feel like you can't breathe. Stress is such a common issue, but its normalcy doesn't diminish how disruptive it can be at every level. It's tempting to think, *Oh, well. Nothing I can do about it!*, but that's not true. We *can* do something about it, and we should:

1. **Ask Jesus for clarity.** Sometimes we let our emotions drive our priorities. Ask the Lord to calm your heart and your mind so you can clearly identify how to order your days. A solid plan makes all the difference.

2. **Stay in constant communication with God.** Stress has a way of making us think we're super self-sufficient even though we're not. As you move through each item on your to-do list, share your frustrations with Jesus, tell Him what's overwhelming you, and ask Him for wisdom. You'll be surprised by how present He is in your challenges.

3. **Be thankful.** You're going to get to the other side of the stress, and when you do, thank Jesus for His help. Active thanksgiving will help you remember the Lord's kindness and faithfulness, and it will remind you that you didn't have to eat the elephant alone. Jesus helped you move through a stressful time, and He will do it again.

And by all means, if feeling stressed becomes the norm instead of the exception, reach out to a trusted counselor, ministry leader, or mentor. You don't have to fight it alone. And remember: the Lord is with you when you face stress and anxiety. Do not fret, and do not fear.

READ PSALM 27:13–14.

1. On a scale of 1 (low) to 5 (high), what's your stress level right now?

2. When you're stressed, does it change your mood or how you interact with other people? Explain that a little bit.

3. What are the things causing the most stress in your life right now? Are you tackling those things head-on? Or are you tempted to procrastinate?

_____

_____

_____

4. What are three simple things you could do today to begin to tackle a stressful deadline or situation?

_____

_____

_____

TODAY'S PRAYER

_____

_____

_____

_____

_____

_____

_____

_____

_____

_____

Day 76

My office at school makes me really happy. When I redecorated it a few years ago, I added a good bit of word art to the walls. Blame it on the fact that I was an English major and love a good, thoughtful phrase, but on the main wall alone there are three exhortations ("Be the exception" is one of them). I would like to tell you that the girls who come into my office receive this encouragement with heartfelt gratitude, but the fact is they like to read my signs to me in gentle, borderline-mocking tones that leave all of us laughing by the end of their routine.

Listen. One thing about working with teenagers is you learn not to take yourself too seriously. Sure, my encouraging signs teeter on the edge of officially cheesy to some, but I'm okay with that. In fact, one of my best friend's daughters has perfected the subdued, soothing voice of a public radio host when she reads my signs (not to mention the book titles on my bookshelves—the nerve!). It is 100 percent all in good fun, but there's one sign that is strictly off limits to the mocking.

Here's what it says: "We all sit under the shade of a tree that someone else planted." I'm not exactly sure who first said it, but, man, is it ever true. To differing degrees, we all sit under the covering of people who have gone before us, and while it's true in a practical, everyday sense (Yay for the person who figured out how to put air conditioning in cars, because that particular piece of "shade" is deeply appreciated!), it's especially true when it comes to our faith.

Think about it. Your life has been changed and influenced by the faithful steps of others. In my own life I could point to many people, including my mama, who taught me how to cook and show hospitality. When I was older my friend Mary Jo welcomed me into her Bible study and taught me so much about being a wife and mother. For the last several years, my friend Anne has been a tremendous source of wisdom and encouragement. My life has been deeply impacted by the consistent care of these women, and it has been a privilege to sit under their covering.

I don't know who has been doing the planting in your life—a family member, a youth group leader, a friend's mom, a teacher, a pastor, or a combination of all the above. But while you can, don't miss the opportunity to notice what has grown tall in their lives—what is thriving and healthy—and don't miss the opportunity to place yourself under the covering of their teaching. Listen to sermons. Go to Bible studies. Download podcasts. Dig into Scripture. Ask questions. Listen like crazy.

Enjoy every minute of being able to sit in the shade of what the Lord has done in others' lives. It is pure grace—a totally undeserved gift.

READ PSALM 145:1–7.

1. Who has done some significant planting in your life? What mentors/teachers/pastors have had a big impact on your spiritual growth?

2. As you are currently growing in your walk with the Lord, who is providing some shade for you to do that? What does that look like?

3. Is it easy or hard for you to ask someone for advice or help? Do you ever find yourself wandering around in the blinding sun (so to speak) because you resist the shade of godly wisdom and counsel?

4. Can you identify a few areas where you're growing stronger and healthier right now? What are they?

TODAY'S PRAYER

Day 77

J grew up in a family that liked to take road trips. I spent large stretches of my childhood summers sprawled out in the back seat of Mama's Ford LTD while Daddy put the country's interstate systems to good use. Sometimes we would drive from my home state of Mississippi to somewhere relatively close, like Arkansas or Oklahoma. But then there was the summer we went from Mississippi all the way to Idaho (we traversed a lot of states, my friends), and another time we road-tripped to Washington, D.C. All that travel meant that for two or three weeks, we were almost entirely out of touch with friends, family, and current events. It was the late seventies or early eighties, so there were no cell phones, satellite radio, or Wi-Fi. We certainly couldn't check in with Mamaw and Papaw, who were back home in Mississippi, via a quick text.

It was a level of disconnection that was disorienting almost. I remember returning home, seeing the stack of newspapers our neighbors had collected for us, and thinking, *There is NO WAY Mama and Daddy will be able catch up on all that news.* As soon as I walked in the back door, I would make a beeline for the phone and call my friend Laura; I couldn't wait to hear the latest happenings from the pool. When it came to trying to get back in the loop, reading the paper and calling a friend were pretty much the only options.

Today, of course, is nothing like that. We are tethered to one another at all times. We can watch the news on our phones or even on an overseas flight (I will never forget boarding an international flight in Kenya and discovering that almost everyone's in-flight screens were tuned to a Senate hearing in the United States). People can snap their friends from the Eiffel Tower if they want; they can send a meme from a gondola as they travel through Venice. It's a level of connection that's almost mind-blowing, and while it certainly has its advantages, I just want to remind us (me too!) of one thing:

Even Jesus needed to disconnect every once in a while.

There are several times in Scripture when Jesus very deliberately moved away from people so that He could be alone. Sometimes it was because He was heartbroken (Matthew 14:10–13), sometimes it was because He needed to pray (Luke 5:16), and sometimes it was because He needed to get ready for what was ahead (Luke 4:1–2). These weren't the only times when He retreated from crowds or distanced Himself from His disciples either, and that tells us something: if solitude was helpful for the Savior of the world, it's good for us too. We don't realize how often we're interrupted by alerts and headlines and texts and notifications; we forget how beneficial it is to read and think and pray without interruption. Sure, we excel at documenting our lives, but it's unlikely that we spend enough time reflecting, praying, processing, and preparing. We are rarely disconnected from one another, and while technology is a wonderful gift, it's a terrible boss.

Look for some time in the next few days—even if it's only for a half hour—when you can put your phone away, eliminate distractions, and focus on the Lord. It might be hard to believe, but disconnection is a grace. It'll be so good for your heart and your head, and it's a wonderful way to follow Jesus' lead.

READ MARK 1:32–38.

1. Does your phone ever get on your nerves? Or do you love having it with you at all times? Explain.

2. How do interruptions make you feel? Do they frustrate you? Or do you like the diversion?

3. How do you feel about time alone? Does it make you uncomfortable to think about intentionally choosing to be away from your friends and family? Or do you wish you had more time without other people around?

4. What's your favorite way to spend uninterrupted time with Jesus? To pray? To read Scripture? To journal? To drive around while you sing worship music? Or to simply be still and quiet? Write about that a little bit.

TODAY'S PRAYER

Day 78

*I*t seems like no matter where I turn right now—particularly in terms of what I read and what I watch—I'm seeing lots of calls for unity. Some people are asking for unity in the church, some are asking for unity in the government, and some are asking for unity in our nation as we face a myriad of challenges. There are also pleas for unity in personal situations. I absolutely appreciate that people see unity as a goal; after all, I'm a nine on the Enneagram—a peace lover—so unity feels like a solid place to land. What we don't always realize, though, is that we can't just decide to be unified, whether it's in our friendships or our churches or our workplaces. That's because unity is a process, not just a feeling. And while true unity is a wonderful thing, it takes hard work to get there.

Here are a few thoughts as you consider the places where you feel compelled to work toward unity in Jesus' name:

1. **Unity requires repentance.** Repentance means that we turn from our sin—whether sinful beliefs, sinful actions, or both—and turn toward God. We often lack unity because of how we've mistreated one another, how we've marginalized one another, and how we've refused to truly listen to one another. If we sincerely want to move in the direction of unity, we have to own our own messes. We have to name them. And we have to turn from them and agree with what God says about those things. Obviously unity would be much easier if we could all just hold hands, sing a worship song, then scream, "WE'RE UNITED NOW!" It's not quite that simple, though.

2. **Unity requires forgiveness.** When people are not unified—when they're not on the same page about a civic issue or theological debate or scientific approach or whatever—they may have intentionally or unintentionally said and done things to hurt people on the other side. This means people will likely need to ask for forgiveness. This means people will need to be willing

to forgive. Unity can't co-exist with bitterness and resentment. Unity can't happen when we're prideful or when we hold people's mistakes over their heads and refuse to forgive them. Forgiveness removes the relational roadblocks that would keep us from moving in the direction of unity—so it's essential to ask for and offer forgiveness when necessary.

3. **Unity requires honesty.** Obviously repentance and forgiveness require us to be honest (and don't forget vulnerable—all of this is really vulnerable!). But to move forward in our families, in our schools, and wherever we're prioritizing unity, we have to *continue* to be honest with one another. We have to speak up if we feel hurt or dismissed by someone. We have to tell the truth when people ask us questions. We can't say something cutting and then pretend like it was a joke. We have to be straightforward and clear as we communicate. No pretending. No posing. No manipulating. And lots of sincere honor and compassion for other people as we bear with one another in love and grace.

True unity is a blessing from God and a reflection of His heart. It's an act of grace to the human race. It takes hard work, but it's worth it—and He is able to help us get there.

READ PSALM 133:1–3.

1. Where are you most aware of a lack of unity? In our country? In a particular community you're part of? In a specific close relationship? Feel free to list more than one thing if you think of several examples.

_____

_____

_____

_____

2. Do you have any personal relationships—either with one other person or with a group of people—that seem to lack unity? What's the disconnect, do you think?

3. Is it difficult for you to ask for someone's forgiveness? Is it difficult for you to forgive someone? Explain that a little bit.

4. Why is being honest often such a challenge in our relationships, communities, and churches? Why do you think we're sometimes willing to pretend instead of telling someone the truth? How do you think this keeps us from true unity?

TODAY'S PRAYER

Day 79

When Alex was five, we experienced our first Christmas without any extended family in our house. My parents were with my brother and his family, my sister and her husband were with his family, and on Christmas Eve, it was just David, Alex, and me. I told myself that I was going to be a grown-up and handle the situation like a champion.

Reader, I did not handle the situation like a champion.

I won't bore you with all the details of how our Christmas Eve went awry, but we ended up having dinner at a Popeye's—the only diners, no less—while the Popeye's employees enjoyed a Christmas party in a far corner of the restaurant. One of the cashiers even shared a sugar cookie with Alex—who was DELIGHTED—but as I have said a thousand times since, one day I'm going to write a children's book about the whole pitiful affair, and I'm going to call it *Santa's Last Drumstick*. You will not convince me otherwise.

Fortunately our extended family rolled into town the day after Christmas, but the big takeaway from that sad Christmas Eve was that our family of three was desperately deficient in the "community" department. You might be able to relate if you've ever been in a situation where you struggled to find a group of close friends. David and I both wanted deep, sincere relationships with other people in our church, but for many reasons it wasn't as easy as we expected.

Several years later we found the close-knit community we had been looking/hoping/praying for. Now we're in a small group, we travel together, we hang out when we can, and three of us even work at the same place. We're committed to magnifying the Lord and exalting His name together (Psalm 34). And over the course of these last several years, we've realized several things about the dynamics of deep friendship in the context of Christian community. You may have experienced the same:

- **Stage One: The Idyllic Phase.** Everyone and everything are wonderful, not to mention hilarious. Clearly every gathering and every meal we share will be marked by quick-witted conversation and well-timed one-liners. Also, our children are angels. Bless the Lord.

- **Stage Two: Reality Sets In.** The shine starts to wear off. We know who struggles with fear, who struggles with pride, who struggles with being super opinionated (RAISING MY HAND). Our parenting challenges could fill a book, and at different points we've been so furious with our spouses that we sat through small group in stony silence. In conversation we say things we regret, or maybe we don't say what we know we should. It's not always easy to be honest and vulnerable.

- **Stage Three: In It to Win It.** Life is hard, but we will walk through it together. We'll take care of each other, look out for each other, pray for each other, and love the Lord together. There are no illusions, and we don't always agree. Sometimes we have difficult conversations. But despite our collective pile of weaknesses, life is better when we witness the Lord's faithfulness together, when we see how He meets us in our struggles when we live for Him together.

Genuine community isn't easy. It can't be superficial, which means it may expose more of your heart than you want people to see. But what grace to be your whole, real self in the presence of fellow believers—without fear of judgment or shame.

READ 1 CHRONICLES 16:23–28.

1. On a scale of 1 (low) to 5 (high), how great do you think your need for sincere, God-honoring community is? Explain.

2. Have you ever experienced "the idyllic phase" in a new friendship or when you found a new group of friends? Describe the feeling.

3. Why do you think people are often tempted to bail when a friendship—or a small group, even—starts to get really real?

4. Why is it helpful (and important!) to have relationships with other believers who see the good, the bad, and the ugly in our lives?

TODAY'S PRAYER

Day 80

When I was a little girl, I thought idols were something that got you in trouble if you worshipped them. The idols in my head were always gold statues or wooden pillars—or maybe even the necklace that jinxed the characters in *The Brady Bunch* when they went to Hawaii (yes, I realize I'm dating myself, but *The Brady Bunch* came on every afternoon when I was in elementary school). I didn't understand the practical function of various idols in my own life, but since I didn't own any gold statues or wooden pillars, I figured I was doing pretty well.

Not so fast, little Sophie.

When I was older and gained some understanding about how idols actually work, I realized that I was practically swimming in a sea of them. IDOLS APLENTY, my friends. And while I could never create an exhaustive list, here are the first ten that come to mind (trust me when I tell you this is barely the tip of the idol iceberg): people's approval, achievements, control, money, food, appearance, writing, my marriage, my child, and my reputation.

At different times I have elevated and served every single one of these things over Jesus. Take the approval of others, for instance. I have elevated it to a place in my life it doesn't belong. I have given it unmerited access to my heart—my sense of worth (and my mood) rising and falling based on what other people think—and, to some degree, I have obeyed that idol. This means instead of asking God what He prefers me to do in a situation, I do whatever will make people the happiest with me.

I'll tell you something else: idols don't fall easily. In fact, if you want to meet some resistance, try confronting an idol head-on. The possibility of losing that idol will make you angry, it will make you defensive, and then, when it finally topples, it will fall hard. You'll resent the fact that it needed to fall in the first place. You'll be tempted to pick up the pieces and see if you can put them back together with superglue. And once you realize that idol is really, truly gone, there will be times when you'll miss it. A lot.

I'm not a person who runs around issuing a lot of spiritual warnings—

mainly because I think fear is a terrible way to try to get people's attention, especially when we're talking about the gospel. I will say this, though: at every stage of your life, as you grow and change in your relationship with the Lord, pay attention to the stuff you're tempted to idolize. Idols are sneaky because they usually start off as something you simply enjoy. What can happen, though, is our affection for those things—or rather, our dependence on those things—gets disordered. Idols cause deep pain in people's lives. It's an area where we need to constantly be on the offensive, asking the Lord (and the people who love us) to alert us when any belief, person, or pursuit is ascending to a place in our hearts and minds that it doesn't deserve. We also need the humility to say, *Uh-oh, I haven't been handling this thing in the best way, but I hear you, Lord.*

You should know that I'm tempted to end today's devotional by reminding you that we can't be idle in dealing with our idols, but clearly, I wouldn't subject you to such a painful pun. (I'm smiling so big right now.) Fight the good fight today, everybody. Our idols are not worth it, but He is worthy.

READ ISAIAH 44:6–8.

1. Why shouldn't we let our idols boss us around? What's the danger with that?

_____

_____

2. Are there any idols you're dealing with right now? Any stuff in your life where you think, *Ummm, I don't think that's meant to be quite this big of a deal?* Write a list here.

_____

_____

_____

3. Take some time to think about how you'd react if someone lovingly confronted you about anything on your list. Do you think you'd be defensive? Breezy? Would you try to diminish the power that thing has in your life?

4. Look up 1 Corinthians 10:14. Write/illustrate/doodle it here.

TODAY'S PRAYER

Day 81

*J*f you have listened to the news recently, then you know how easy it is to hear about everything going on in the world and feel overwhelmed. Tensions run high between countries, people disagree about how to address all manner of social issues, and currently, there's much debate about the management of a global pandemic. If you added two hundred more current events to this list, it would still be incomplete—and that's precisely why it's so easy to observe what's going on in the world and feel confused about how to help. There's uncertainty, discord, and confusion, and as believers who want to see "[His] Kingdom come, [His] will be done, on earth as it is in heaven" (Matthew 6:10), we might be tempted to look around and say, *I'm not so sure that we're making a whole lot of forward progress, everybody.*

So in case you haven't thought about it lately, maybe this reminder will encourage you: God is so *big.* And I don't just mean that in a singsongy, "He's got the whole world in His hands" kind of way. I mean it in an Isaiah 40 kind of way. Just look at verses 21–22:

> *Do you not know?*
> *Have you not heard?*
> *Has it not been declared to you*
> *from the beginning?*
> *Have you not considered*
> *the foundations of the earth?*
> *God is enthroned above the circle of the earth;*
> *its inhabitants are like grasshoppers.*

So, first of all, hello, grasshopper. And second of all, look at the *awe* in Isaiah's tone. He starts with four rhetorical questions that sound a little bit like "COME ON, PEOPLE." Then he reminds us that God is not just in heaven; He is on His throne. (Feel free to clap.) All of us—while beloved and created by our heavenly Father—are incredibly small in the grand scheme of things. But even in our relative smallness, we are not helpless, and we are most certainly not hopeless.

When the world gets overwhelming, we're sometimes tempted to assume there's nothing we can do, we'll never make a difference, and we're just one tiny grasshopper-person in a ginormous (official term of measurement) world. But God's bigness compared to our smallness is not an excuse for inaction. We don't get to look at the hurt and heartache around us, sit back, fold our (little grasshopper) arms, and respond with, "Oh well, it's all terrible, but God is sovereign!" Because while it's true that God is sovereign, *we have to be responsible.* We are Christ's ambassadors on this planet (2 Corinthians 5:20), so we have work to do! Micah 6:8 says God intends for us "to act justly, to love faithfulness, and to walk humbly with [Him]." We're not meant to be bystanders, so we want to get after it and be people who are loving, compassionate agents of hope and change in Jesus' name. That's why it's essential for us to be mindful of the might and the power and the strength of the One who calls us to love and serve—because ultimately, we're dependent on Him, not ourselves. As Isaiah 40:29 says, "He gives strength to the faint and strengthens the powerless." We'll need every bit of that.

Yes, there are times when it feels like the world is screaming. But even in the midst of the chaos, Jesus holds. And by the grace and power of the Holy Spirit, we get to carry His peace and His deep affection for people with us wherever we go. We get to change the world. Get after it, grasshoppers.

READ ISAIAH 40:21–26.

1. Do you feel a responsibility to know what's going on in the world around you? How do you stay aware of both the needs in your community and the needs in the world?

2. Have you ever felt compelled to serve in a certain way? To volunteer for a local organization? To travel on a mission trip? To get involved in your neighborhood? Did you follow through? If you haven't served yet, is that something you would like to do eventually? Explain.

3. What are some ways you could love and minister to the brokenhearted? To be clear, we're all broken, but in this instance, I'm speaking of needs you see in your community, church, city, etc.

4. Why do you think we're so tempted to look the other way when we're confronted with heartache, hard stories, and division in our communities?

TODAY'S PRAYER

Day 82

*O*ne of the things we try to do pretty regularly at my school (twice a year, at least) is set aside time for our junior high girls to ask our senior girls questions. Generally I'll set a loose theme for our time together ("relationships," "managing stress," "battling perfectionism," etc.), and then the junior high girls will submit questions to me. I'll ask five or six senior girls to sit on a panel, and then on the designated day, we'll spend thirty or thirty-five minutes in the auditorium while the senior girls answer the questions for an audience of seventh- and eighth-grade girls.

Y'all. It literally takes fifteen minutes to put together one of these Q&A sessions—they're super low maintenance to plan—and I am always shocked by the response to them. The girls, both younger and older, love them. They look forward to them. They stop me in the hall and ask when we can have another one. And when the senior girls answer the junior high girls' questions, you could hear a pin drop in that auditorium. We always involve senior girls who represent a wide range of interests and activities, so the junior high girls are listening to older, wiser athletes, band members, student leaders, and more. The senior girls don't think much about it, but because of their age and the ways they've been involved at school, they've established some authority in the younger girls' lives.

So here's my encouragement to you today: even though you probably can't fathom that anyone looks up to you, there are *most definitely* people who look up to you. There are girls a few years behind you—young women in your school or church or neighborhood—who notice how you treat people. They notice how you laugh with your friends. They think you're courageous because you run cross-country or you work two part-time jobs or you just got accepted to med school. They wish they knew you well enough to borrow that gorgeous dress you wore in your brother's wedding. (They saw it because they follow you on Instagram.) (Of course.)

They wonder how you get your hair to look like that, how you felt on your first date, how you deal with anxiety, and how you get along with your mom. They wonder who you talk to when things are hard. They wonder if you've ever been lonely and how you recovered when a friend broke your heart. They wonder if there will ever be an end to friend drama. (I'll go ahead and tell you: they can't imagine that the answer to that question is no.) They wonder if your real life matches the highlight reel they see on social media. They wonder what it looks like for you to love and follow Jesus and if you would tell them that He's worth it.

None of this means you have to be perfect—I promise. In fact, how you deal with your mistakes and setbacks can be super influential in younger girls' lives. But for better or worse, as those younger girls are trying to figure out who they want to be, they're looking at you. They may be five years younger, and after you move into the next phase of your life, you may never see them again. But right now those girls are your neighbors. They see you—sometimes up close but mostly from afar. And they will remember you.

Consider today how you can encourage younger girls who look up to you. Love your neighbors well.

READ MATTHEW 22:35–39.

1. When you were younger, who were the older girls you looked up to and wanted to imitate?

_____

_____

_____

2. Who do you look up to right now? Why?

_____

_____

_____

3. How can it impact our decisions and actions if we remember that younger girls are watching us?

_____

_____

_____

4. If you had the opportunity to give a group of younger girls three pieces of advice, what would they be? Explain them a little bit.

_____

_____

_____

_____

TODAY'S PRAYER

_____

_____

_____

_____

_____

_____

_____

_____

_____

_____

_____

Day 83

*M*y friend Melanie and I often laugh about the expression "since the dawn of time." The phrase usually signals that we're having trouble describing something—or we can't break down the nuances of a particular problem— so our go-to generality is that people have struggled with that issue "since the dawn of time." The truth is that many of our daily struggles seem like they've been around for about that long. Whether we're dealing with body image, relationship frustrations, or a nagging sense that we're not sure who to trust, there's nothing new under the sun, right?

Without question one of the biggest since-the-dawn-of-time issues is racism. It's a part of every nation's history, and it continues to rear its ugly head in the present day. It's often a difficult topic to talk about because emotions can get so heated, but people who profess Jesus as their Savior need to be especially clear about this: mistreating people because of their racial or ethnic backgrounds—and being unwilling to take responsibility when it comes to genuine repentance and the pursuit of peace—is a distorted reflection of the heart of Jesus. Racism is not only a cancer in our society; it's a blight on the body of Christ. It has absolutely no place in the church.

So what does that mean for believers? It means we need to take an unflinching inventory of where we see racism, not only in our own thoughts and actions, but also in our communities. And when we notice where even the tiniest seedlings of racism have taken root, we need to deal with them by confessing our wrong belief and asking the Lord to help us see people as He does. Not a single one of us has the right to diminish the value of other people for any reason—and certainly not because of the color of their skin. In fact, advocating for the honor, worth, and dignity of every single person should be a place where Christians lead boldly, clearly, and without compromise. Period.

What we forget sometimes, I think, is that diversity here on earth is a glimpse of what heaven will be like. In Revelation 7, John had a vision where "there was a vast multitude from every nation, tribe, people, and language, which no one could number, standing before the throne and before the Lamb" (v. 9). This is the Kingdom to come. As believers, we have been called to establish a foretaste of that Kingdom right here, right now. A world where everyone looks the same, speaks the same, and shares the same culture has never been the end goal of Christianity.

By God's grace we have endless opportunities to love and learn from all sorts of people—people He created with great intention, I would add. But if we let our preconceived (or flat-out sinful) judgments and biases keep us away from the beautiful kaleidoscope of humanity the Lord has made, we'll miss countless opportunities to show the world what He's about. As people who profess Jesus as Lord, we should never be willing to sacrifice our public witness on the altar of private prejudice. Racism has no place in the Kingdom of God, and it has no place in the heart and mind of a believer.

Lead boldly and clearly today by affirming the inherent dignity of "every nation, tribe, people, and language" with your words and your actions. This is the work of heaven on earth.

READ EPHESIANS 2:14–18.

1. How would you define racism? Why does racism grieve the heart of God?

2. Why do you think some people are defensive when the topic of racism is introduced? What makes people resistant to honest self-examination in this area?

3. Spend some time thinking and praying about moments when you've been aware of your own prejudices and biases or when you've suffered as the result of someone else's. Have you ever talked to the Lord about those moments? Write out whatever you need to say to Him.

_____

_____

_____

4. What's the state of your own heart right now regarding racism? Are you angry? Apathetic? Bitter? Broken? Explain.

_____

_____

_____

TODAY'S PRAYER

_____

_____

_____

_____

_____

_____

_____

_____

_____

_____

Day 84

I will confess that there are days when I truly believe I can read my dog's mind. I don't know exactly what leads to my perception of such a deep level of familiarity, but sometimes she'll pace by the front door and I'll think, *Oh, bless her. She's ready for her daddy to get home.* There are other times when she follows my every early-morning move, and I'll think, *Poor Hazel. She doesn't want me to go to work today.* Granted, I'm not all that familiar with the thought processes of a seven-year-old mutt who is gifted in separation anxiety, but apparently, I'm totally comfortable with making a lot of assumptions about Hazel's feelings.

Late one afternoon a couple of weeks ago, Hazel just wasn't acting like herself. She seemed restless for one thing (Hazel is very gifted at sleeping), and she didn't want to hang out with me (Hazel typically finds my company to be delightful). I worried about her for several hours, and before long I realized that I was trying to read her mind. *She's probably still upset that we took her to the vet a couple of days ago; I could tell that she was mad at me when I picked her up.* As it turned out, Hazel's issues were physical, not emotional (imagine that). She had an upset stomach, and while she didn't feel great for the next several hours, she was back to her normal self in no time at all.

You don't have to tell me how ridiculous every bit of this is because TRUST ME, I GET IT. While reflecting on my misguided attempts to READ THE MIND OF A DOG, I realized I do the exact same thing with people. For example, I'll get a brief reply to a lengthy email and think, *She's probably still annoyed with me for that dumb thing I said yesterday at lunch.* Lots of us do this, I think. Maybe a friend doesn't look up from her phone when you walk past her between classes, and your go-to reaction is, *I bet I freaked her out when I talked forever about my summer breakup, and she doesn't want to be my friend anymore.*

The reality, of course, is that she was just looking at her phone. It had absolutely nothing to do with the story about the breakup. But so many times—way too often, in fact—we ascribe motive where there's absolutely no motive. We feel unsettled by the way someone acts/reacts/responds, and we immediately want to figure out that whole thing. We want to identify cause and effect so we can make our peace with whatever horrible relational reality awaits us—even when that imagined reality involves a dog with PTSD.

The solution here is not to think more about other people so that we can keep everyone happy. The solution is to think of ourselves less. We don't always associate our need to immediately figure out a perceived problem as selfishness, but oftentimes it is. We are not the cause of everyone's heartache. We are not the center of everyone's universe. People have whole, complete moods that have absolutely nothing to do with us. And while our intentions are probably good, we have to remember that there's a fine line between being compassionate and being codependent. Even with our dogs, apparently.

Sometimes friends just have bad days. Show some grace to them and to yourself. Resist the urge to "read their mind." Just love them right where they are.

READ 1 PETER 1:22–23.

1. When a friend is upset, how often do you assume it's because of something you did (or didn't do)?

_____

_____

2. Is perceived conflict with a friend difficult for you to manage emotionally? Or do you tend to assume there's no problem until someone tells you there's a problem? Explain that a little bit.

_____

_____

3. Can you think of a situation where you were looking to people for emotional security instead of looking to God? How did that work out? What did you learn?

4. Are you ever tempted to try to read someone's mind or predict what's going on when you perceive distance or change in a relationship? Why is that almost always a bad idea?

TODAY'S PRAYER

Day 85

At this point I've spent most of my adult life working in ministry. For the longest time that work was in classrooms where I taught English. Then, about seven years ago, I shifted to a job where I primarily talked and listened to high school girls. I feel like I've witnessed just about every form of disappointment, heartache, and heartbreak, and I've also witnessed the Lord at work in the most tender, miraculous, personal ways. I can't begin to tell you how many times an administrator or a parent has asked me to have a conversation with someone—and then, minutes later, that very person has stopped by my office for some seemingly random reason.

It was never actually random, of course. Seeing how intricately the Lord arranges circumstances to fight for the hearts of His children has truly been the privilege of a lifetime. I will never get over what I've seen Him do.

There have also, of course, been times of deep discouragement. There have been times when I sat in the parking lot before work and thought, *Lord, I don't know if I can go in that building today.* There have been misunderstandings I may never get to mend, there have been instances where my pride made me super ineffective, and there have been days I put my head on my desk and cried after a girl left my office. I'd like to think that through the highs and lows of all these experiences, I've learned how to care for people well, but I don't know. For one thing I'm pretty stinkin' human, and for another thing, I can start to feel pretty stinkin' self-sufficient.

Earlier this week, in fact, I was feeling really self-sufficient (and probably pretty self-righteous, honestly)—sharing some work-related thoughts and feelings with a close friend—when conviction hit me right in the gut: *When I'm at work, am I performing? Or am I surrendering to the Holy Spirit?*

I mean, after all these years, I feel like I understand how to express concern, how to react without shock or judgment, and how to comfort and challenge with words that reflect the Truth of Scripture. But I don't ever want to just go through the motions. In every situation I want to depend on the leading of the Holy Spirit; I want to be mindful that self-sufficiency has no place in my life as a believer.

You may not need this reminder as much as I have this week, but I want to share it: God isn't asking any of us to put on a show of faith in Jesus' name. When we're mid-struggle, or when we're feeling conviction in a certain area, or when we're wrestling with how to handle a tricky situation, we can talk to God. He will hear us. His power will be made perfect in our weakness (2 Corinthians 12:9). We don't have to solve everything ourselves within the next twenty-four hours.

So this is grace: even when we feel like we're a little bit of a hot mess—when we're smack-dab in the middle of working something out with the Lord—He will not leave us. He is faithful. By the power of the Holy Spirit, He is with us in our conviction, in our uncertain circumstances, and in our doubt. He will continue to teach us. He will show us the way.

READ ROMANS 8:1–6.

1. Is there an area where you're feeling convicted regarding your faith? Explain that a little.

_____

_____

_____

2. Can you think of a situation when you felt like you were performing or going through the motions as a believer?

_____

_____

_____

3. Fill in the blank: Lord, I'm really struggling with _____ _____. Will You please help me _____ _____?

4. Are you hoping that the Lord will settle a particular situation in your head and your heart? Is there a situation where you are feeling especially dependent on Him right now? Describe it.

TODAY'S PRAYER

Day 86

It's not the most elegant metaphor, but I hope you'll bear with me: lately I've been thinking about how a life of faith reminds me of a relay race. There's stuff that we inherit, stuff that we carry around like a baton, and stuff we pass on to the person who's running the leg after us. (The metaphor breaks down a bit when we think about running side by side with others—or running at the same time with one of us slightly ahead—but for the time being, let's consider running with a figurative baton. Let's think about what we've picked up and what we're passing on.)

Over and over in Scripture, younger and older people enjoy some overlap in their assignments from God. They're sharing a baton, so to speak. Whether we're talking about Lois and Eunice training Timothy in the faith, Moses and Joshua leading the Israelites out of exile, or Naomi and Ruth seeking the redemption of their family line, there's a pattern of teaching and learning, establishing and inheriting, passing on and picking up. All of these things are in the service of working—or running, as it were—for something much bigger than personal glory. All of these things are for the glory of God.

Obviously we're not living in biblical times, but each one of us is definitely running a race of faith (Hebrews 12:1). Each one of us is carrying a baton that's full of what has been passed on to us, and sometimes it's good to rest for a minute and consider what's inside that baton. Is it getting heavy? Are we carrying bits and pieces of someone's bitterness and baggage without realizing it? Have people unknowingly passed on biases or bad theology? Are our races labored and difficult because we're continuing to carry what needs to be laid down?

More than that: as we consider what we no longer want or need to carry, let's also consider what we want to hold on to and hand off to someone else. Let's consider what good we can add to those batons. My guess is we'll find them easier to carry—and then pass on—if we add the things that truly reflect the heart of our Savior. After all, Jesus says when we come to Him, our burden becomes lighter (Matthew 11:30). So if we're running with batons filled to the brim with compassion, love, mercy, grace, and peace that only come from Jesus, we'll run more freely in our own races, AND we'll better equip the people who are running behind us. Finally, we'll be better teammates because we won't be weighed down by carrying a bunch of stuff we don't actually need.

I know. This is a lot of language about running from someone who much prefers walking. But man oh man, it sure is helpful to not only think about how we're running this race called life but also to consider what we're carrying. To spend time thinking about what we'd like to pass on to the people running behind us. Maybe it's someone you lead in Bible study, or someone you mentor in college, or a niece, daughter, or eventual great-grandchild.

Remember: you're not running your race in isolation. You're running with what you've picked up and what you'll be passing on. You're not running your race just for yourself. You're running for the glory of God. Run well today, my friend.

READ PSALM 78:1-4.

1. Consider the hypothetical baton we've been talking about today. What have you inherited from people who have gone before you in the faith? From people who have been influential in your walk with the Lord? What are you carrying?

2. At this current stage of running your race of faith, how do you feel? Is the running difficult? Do you feel weighed down? Are you winded? Tired? Or are you mostly running freely?

3. Is there anything in that baton (so to speak) that needs to go? Anything that isn't helpful as you run right now?

4. What are five things you want to be sure to put in your baton so that you can pass them on? Why are those things important to your life of faith? What do they mean to you?

TODAY'S PRAYER

Day 87

$\mathcal{S}$he was sitting on the other side of my desk. Wide-eyed, she was exasperated by my most recent question. We had been talking about her relationship with a guy she cared about, and when I wondered aloud why she continued to respond in certain ways (I know that's vague, but the particulars aren't my story to tell—you understand), she exhaled with the force of a small hurricane and spoke in what felt like all caps.

MRS. HUDSON. EVERYTHING DOESN'T HAVE TO MEAN SOMETHING. WHY DO YOU ALWAYS THINK THERE'S SOMETHING DEEPER GOING ON? I JUST REACT THE WAY I REACT. WHY DOES IT HAVE TO BE A BIG DEAL?

She exhaled again, this time ushering in some calm: *I don't think there's some big lesson in all of this. It just is what it is.*

Five or six years later, the two of us met for lunch. She caught me up on some significant developments in her life and her relationship with the Lord, and out of nowhere, she said something along the lines of, *Hey, I know I used to give you a hard time about digging for the deeper meaning in my decisions. But now I think there really was something to that. I've been able to see how a lot of my struggles were the result of one particular issue.* Then she continued to catch me up on her life, I continued to eat my salad, and we didn't say much more about it.

As I have reflected more on that conversation, I am astounded by the grace of the Lord toward my friend. In high school she couldn't see there was a pattern at work in her decision-making, primarily in her relationships with guys—but she sees it now.

My struggle or your struggle might be different, but all of us will battle destructive patterns because, well, we are sinners. Typically there's something bossing us around as we wrestle with those patterns—whether it's fear or insecurity or a lie we've come to believe—and that bossy voice gets so loud we can literally know we're doing the wrong thing, but we fully commit to it anyway. The apostle Paul was all too familiar with this struggle; in Romans 7:15 he said, "I do not practice what I want to do, but I do what I hate."

We are not hopeless or helpless, however. Just as the Lord enabled my friend to see what was going on underneath the surface of her decisions, He can do the same for us. Scripture reminds us that "we are not obligated to the flesh to live according to the flesh" (Romans 8:12). We can ask the Lord to show us, by the power of the Holy Spirit, where (and why) we're caught in a pattern that isn't God's best for us. Whether that pattern affects our thoughts, our decisions, our actions, or all of the above, we are not powerless against it! The Lord can help us see that thing for what it really is—and see it clearly.

Even when you feel like you're stuck in a pattern you don't understand, the grace of God will make a way out (1 Corinthians 10:13). Pay attention to all the ways He's at work in your life today. He loves you more than you know.

READ ROMANS 8:7–11.

1. Do you see any patterns in your life that could be problematic down the road? It could be people pleasing, withdrawing from people, persistent relational drama, making impulsive decisions, engaging in risky behavior, etc.

2. When you're caught in one of these patterns, how do you feel? Are you numb? Does it feel normal? Write about that a little bit.

3. Have you recently done something you didn't want to do? What were the circumstances surrounding your decision? Were you persuaded by people? Were you motivated by fear? Explain.

_____

_____

_____

4. Look up the song "Way Maker" by Sinach. Write the chorus here, and afterward, write down two or three areas/patterns where you're asking the Lord to make a way today.

_____

_____

_____

_____

TODAY'S PRAYER

_____

_____

_____

_____

_____

_____

_____

_____

Day 88

I am what you might call a Certified Clumsy Individual. If there's an opportunity to trip, stumble, or fall flat on my face, I will find it. I am also pretty skilled at accidentally burning myself and dropping random objects in a disruptive manner. In the last few months alone, I rolled my right ankle on a crab apple (this ankle, bless it, has already suffered more injuries than any joint should be forced to endure), I have seared two fingers while cooking steaks in a cast-iron skillet (here's a tip: hot butter splatters everywhere), and I have broken a toe because I started walking without realizing where the chair leg was.

I'm the embodiment of effortless poise and elegance, if you haven't noticed.

My most recent display of spectacular clumsiness was about a month ago. When I came home from dinner with friends, Hazel was, as always, ecstatic to see me. Usually she shows some initial enthusiasm and then backs away, but on this particular night, Hazel remained all up in my personal space. I was trying to make my way to the half bath by our kitchen, but when I tried to step over her, Hazel tried to keep up with me, and then I accidentally stepped on the edge of one of her paws, and then she yelped and my feet got very, I don't know, *intertwined*. The next thing I knew, I was falling forward in what seemed to be slow motion, trying to figure out the best way not to twist my already much-maligned right ankle in the process.

My solution? I bent my knees and let them take the brunt of the impact. On one hand, YAY, ME! I SAVED MY ANKLE! On the other hand, YEOW, KNEES. The pain rolled in so quickly that I stayed put for about thirty seconds, face-down on the floor, while I tried to figure out my next best move. My husband asked if he could help, but in addition to being clumsy, I AM STUBBORN. So I eventually settled for crawling into the bathroom and pulling myself to my feet by using the countertop as a brace. It was a *super* dignified moment. Also, my knees hurt for the next six days.

The truth of the matter is, both physically and spiritually, we all fall down sometimes. (Yes, I have fully transitioned to the spiritual application of this devotion.) It's not that we want, plan, or hope to. We just do. We mess up. We don't look where we're going. We get burned by something that seemed too far away to hurt us. We turn left when we should have turned right. And this is your official reminder that when we fall down—whether it's the result of our inattentiveness or the fact that something else tripped us—we can, by the grace of God, respond in three ways:

1. **Get back up again (Psalm 37:24).** No mistake gets to hold us forever.

2. **Let people help us (Galatians 6:1).** I admit that it's difficult for me to admit my need for help. It's the best way, though.

3. **Rest in God's forgiveness (Psalm 103:12).** He has more grace and mercy for us than we can ever comprehend.

Unfortunately, there will always be opportunities to stumble as we walk through life. Thankfully, though, God's grace covers us even when we fall. In the meantime, watch where you're going, everybody. Be careful out there.

READ PSALM 46:1–7.

1. Do you think of yourself as a clumsy person? Why or why not? No judgment if you're, like, super elegant and have never tripped in public.

2. Have you ever experienced a significant stumble in your walk with the Lord? What did that look like? How did you get back up again?

3. Have you ever had the opportunity to help or encourage a friend who has (figuratively) fallen down and was having a hard time? What did that experience teach you?

4. Look up Psalm 46:1. Write/doodle/illustrate it here.

TODAY'S PRAYER

Day 89

J was walking into work when I realized what was happening. It was a normal Tuesday—nothing unusual on that day's calendar—but as soon as I felt the all-too-familiar pressure in the top of my chest, I knew that my body didn't get the memo about it being a stress-free day. That pressure in my chest is always the first signal that anxiety intends to keep me company for at least part of the day, and over the last several years, I have become all too familiar with what follows: the shortened breath, then, sometimes, a pulse rate that makes me wonder if my heart is trying to break free from my body.

Honestly, I'm tempted to make light of the whole anxiety attack phenomenon (HUMOR MAKES THINGS EASIER, RIGHT?), but I don't want in any way to diminish the fact that it's something a whole bunch of us deal with. Also, it can be scary on several levels. For one thing, the first time it happens, you have absolutely no idea what's going on with your body. Then there's the fear that you'll have to deal with the anxiety forever—the fear that there's no end in sight. And on top of that, there's the additional anxiety that your friends or family won't understand, that they'll somehow think differently of you when they learn how you're struggling.

So, for the record, not a single bit of the anxiety-related stuff is fun. However, analyzing can be instructive. I can say with great honesty that the Lord continues to teach me as I work to better understand and manage my anxiety. I hope these things will encourage you, too:

1. **Processing my anxiety prompts me to consider if I've been trying to manage or control something that ultimately belongs to the Lord.** When I examine the root of my anxiety, I sometimes realize that I'm either holding on to anger or bitterness, or I'm trying to control the outcome of a specific situation. None of these are my job.

2. **Processing my anxiety makes me slow down.** Initially, at least, anxiety makes me feel like everything is urgent. This is a lie, of

course. And while I don't exactly understand why it helps so much, I have learned that taking time to write out what I need to do—and in what order—helps me manage any immediate next steps in a more productive way.

3. **Processing my anxiety reminds me to pray.** Scripture tells us to cast our cares on the Lord because He cares for us (1 Peter 5:7). So when I feel anxious, I remember that God can handle it. So whether I go for a walk (which also helps) and talk to Him along the way, or I sit at my desk, close my eyes, and focus my attention on Him for ten or fifteen minutes, He is my safest place. Scripture says that when we are filled with anxiety, His comfort brings us joy (Psalm 94:19). This is such relief.

If you struggle with anxiety, I hope you'll talk to your loved ones (and your doctor and/or counselor) about the best ways to manage it. And if you don't struggle with anxiety, I hope you know how much your care and concern mean to your friends and family members who do. No matter what you're facing today, I pray that you see evidence of God's grace upon grace all around you. He is with you, and He is at work!

READ MATTHEW 11:28–30.

1. Do you ever feel anxious? Does it happen frequently or just every once in a while?

2. Why do you think anxiety is a battle for so many? Do you think people are more likely to talk about it now than they were ten or fifteen years ago? Why do you think that is?

3. When we feel anxious, we don't feel at peace. Whether you struggle with anxiety or not, what other things interfere with your peace? Conflict? Busyness? Other people's expectations? Explain that a little bit.

4. Look up 2 Thessalonians 3:16. Write/doodle/illustrate it here.

TODAY'S PRAYER

Day 90

*A*t the beginning of January, my friend Melanie and I had a conversation on our podcast about what we'd like to do differently in the new year. Neither of us is really in the habit of making big, sweeping resolutions, but since last year was not exactly the easiest, it seemed right and good to think about how this year could potentially be better. For a few minutes neither of us could come up with anything worthwhile, but then I realized I had something resembling a goal forming in the back of my mind. So I blurted it out:

"I'd like to read more books!" I said.

As it turned out, Melanie also wanted to read more books this year, and after a few minutes of discussion about our very ordinary aspirations, (Seriously, for two authors who also happen to LOVE books, reading more should be a piece of cake!), the phrase #lowlevelgoals was born. Sure, you could shoot for the stars at the beginning of a new year, or you could do what Melanie suggested and just shoot for the horizon. I mentioned that shooting for the lowest tree branch might be fine, too, but I'd hate for my lack of ambition to hold anyone back.

For several days our listeners shared their #lowlevelgoals on Instagram, and they were fantastic. One person wanted to be in her pajamas by 8:30 every night. Someone else pledged to make more cookies; another listener vowed to get her glasses fixed. One of my favorites came from a person who wanted to spend more quality time with her dog. And here's the unexpected kicker: even though we never intended it, Melanie and I have actually felt a certain degree of accomplishment with our #lowlevelgoals. We are both making excellent progress on the book-reading front. Who knew we would feel so accomplished over such small victories?

I think there's also something to this kind of approach when it comes to our relationship with the Lord. So often—and as a result of really good intentions—we set Great Big Goals for God. We set out to memorize the entire book of Galatians. We sign up to volunteer in the children's ministry AND sing in the choir AND lead a Bible study. We set the alarm to wake up an hour early so that we can have an extra-long quiet time every morning.

To be clear, every single one of these goals is beautiful and worthwhile. But anyone who actually followed through with all of them would be straight-up exhausted. As Beth Moore once said, "We can't do 1000 things to the glory of God."[5] So while nothing we do for Jesus will technically qualify as "low level" (He is always of high importance), the #lowlevelgoals *mentality* can be really helpful as we grow in our relationship with Him. With this approach, we identify a few places where we want to increase our knowledge, discipline, or service, and we focus on those areas for a while. This reminds us that it takes time and patience for spiritual fruit to develop.

Grace says you don't have to do everything at once. And believe it or not, there's also grace in #lowlevelgoals, which can help us develop healthy, long-lasting habits. Ask the Lord to direct your focus as you seek to love and serve Him little by little!

READ PROVERBS 2:1–6.

1. There's an old saying that "slow and steady wins the race." How does that apply to what we've talked about today? How do #lowlevelgoals relate to that?

_____

_____

_____

_____

_____

5. Beth Moore (@BethMooreLPM), Twitter, June 29, 2020, 8:47 a.m., https://twitter.com/BethMooreLPM/status/1277599503328186368.

2. Where do you land when it comes to goal setting? Do you tend to set ambitious, detailed goals? Or do you try to avoid goals altogether? Why is that, do you think?

3. In terms of the everyday, task-oriented part of your life, what are a couple of #lowlevelgoals that might be helpful?

4. In terms of your relationship with the Lord, what are a couple of #lowlevelgoals (with High Importance!) that might help you grow stronger and wiser spiritually?

TODAY'S PRAYER

Day 91

*W*hen Alex was a baby—just a cuddly little chunk of love who fit snugly in his stroller's basket seat—I would see moms with older kids and 100 percent feel sorry for them. I couldn't imagine what could possibly be enjoyable about life with opinionated, messy teenagers, and I pretty much dreaded the day it would be my reality. I would inevitably gaze back at four-month-old Alex—sound asleep in his stroller—and secretly wish that he never had to grow up.

So here's what I want to tell you about that now that Alex is seventeen.

This phase of parenting has hands down been my favorite. I love everything about it except for the occasional bad attitudes. (Alex has his moments too.) There are so many things to talk about and laugh about, not to mention that this is prime time for parents and kids to figure out what they have in common. For example, it turns out Alex and I share similar tastes in music. You have no idea how this delights me. And a couple of years ago, when Alex and I went to a Ben Rector concert together, well, it was one of my top five favorite memories—and not just because I got to hear some awesome music with Alex.

The night of the concert we arrived about forty-five minutes before showtime. We found our seats, and eventually our friends arrived. We arranged our seating so that Stephanie and Joey sat next to me (David was at home since Alex and I were having a Mama-Son Night), and Alex sat with their daughter, Ella—one of his very best friends—in the row right behind us. This adjustment worked out well for Ella and Alex because they could pretend not to know us if we sang or danced or moved or breathed in any way that was potentially embarrassing to them. And I trust you know I had every intention of BREAKING IT ON DOWN.

At 9:00 p.m. the house lights went down, the stage lights went up, and Ben Rector started to sing. It's safe to say that from the front row to the back row—from the floor level to the second balcony—we were all captivated. From the opening song to the closing one, we all sang our hearts out. We laughed and "awwwww"ed and swayed and clapped. We even followed instructions a few times. It was magical.

About halfway through the show, as our fearless leader-singer-songwriter Ben Rector sat at the piano and sang "Sometime," I choked back unexpected tears for the most unexpected reason. *He wasn't afraid to do something beautiful, I thought. He showed up, and he invited us to join him, and now we've all gotten to be a part of a really meaningful, inspiring evening.*

God's grace is often obvious to us when we're thinking about His unconditional love in the midst of our sinfulness. But it is also the grace of God when we get to enjoy something beautiful with people we love, when we're moved to tears by the ways God has gifted someone, or when we experience the joy of a singer-songwriter from Oklahoma shining some serious light in a dark theater in Birmingham, Alabama.

Was Ben Rector evidence of God's grace that night? You better believe it. And I will never, ever forget it.

READ PSALM 111:1–4.

1. What do you and your mom or dad have in common? What interests do you share?

_____

_____

_____

2. Have you ever found yourself in tears at a live event? What was meaningful to you about it? Why do you think it moved you?

_____

_____

_____

3. What is a recent everyday occurrence that has reminded you of God's grace? A sunset? The sound of laughter? Something else?

_____

_____

_____

4. What are some everyday graces that surround you right now? Make a list of four or five. If you're feeling creative, draw them.

_____

_____

_____

_____

TODAY'S PRAYER

_____

_____

_____

_____

_____

_____

_____

_____

_____

_____

Day 92

It was our fourth day in Nairobi when we found out we'd be visiting a church overlooking the Rift Valley. Alex and I had traveled to Kenya with Compassion International, and we'd been there just long enough to know that if we were visiting an overlook, we'd likely have to travel rough terrain in a safari vehicle. We were right about that. Mercifully, our trip was only about twenty minutes long, and as our driver parked our van along the exterior wall of the church property, we could hear that something was going on before we could actually see it.

People were singing—where, exactly, we couldn't tell—but as we moved closer to the church gates, the voices grew louder. Finally, as we turned the corner, we saw about forty women dancing in a loose formation, moving in our direction, singing worship songs at the top of their lungs. Each woman was wearing a colorful cape tied around her neck, but more noticeable than the capes were the smiles. They were beaming as they welcomed us, and as they moved closer, I could tell that most of them were carrying a baby on their backs. Some were also carrying toddlers in their arms.

The women grabbed our elbows and pulled us into their group, patiently showing us how to move our feet and arms as we sang our way to the church door. We eventually danced into the sanctuary, giddy from the welcome and the joy of being united in worship. A lady named Mary was in charge of Compassion International's work at that particular church. When she stood up to explain what our day would hold, she greeted us on behalf of the church, recounted how the women had led us in worship from the second we stepped on church grounds, and said something I'll never forget: "In Kenya, we hope you know that you are welcome at the gate."

It hit me in the dead center of my heart.

Here's what Mary's words compel me to remember: when we're walking through a figurative gate in our lives—whether that's a change in perspective, a change from high school to college, a change from college to career, a change in age, life stage, or whatever—the Lord is working. He's teaching. He's not just changing our circumstances; He's changing *us*. After all, when we look at gates in Scripture, it's clear that they were places where *things were happening*, whether that was Boaz's redemption of Ruth (Ruth 3), Mordecai's discovery of an assassination plot (Esther 2), or Abraham's purchase of Sarah's tomb (Genesis 23). Things were *settled* at gates in Scripture: community matters, personal matters, even judicial matters were addressed, argued, and decided at the gate.

The same is true right here, right now—just in a metaphorical sense. So maybe, just maybe, as we're fretting and flailing and wondering what might be on the other side, we're missing a much more important idea:

God has invited us to another gate.
And we are welcome.
We can enter the gate with singing.
And God will settle some things when we get there.

READ ISAIAH 26:1–4.

1. Do you typically like change? Or do you resist it?

_____

_____

2. When you think about the metaphorical "gates" in your life—the transitions from one place to another—does it make you excited? Anxious? A little fearful? Explain that.

_____

_____

_____

3. Consider the notion that you're *welcome* at whatever gate might be ahead. Does that change how you feel? Why or why not?

4. Looking back, can you identify how the Lord was at work at previous gates in your life? What did you see Him do? Do you feel like He settled some things?

TODAY'S PRAYER

Day 93

*N*ot too long ago I invited some friends over to celebrate my husband's birthday. Our friends brought their kids—along with one kid's boyfriend that we all adore—and for the first thirty minutes after everyone got to the house, the noise level was OFF THE CHARTS. Even though we have a living room and a den that are perfectly enjoyable places to sit, our guests crammed into the kitchen, and it seemed like everyone was talking loud at once. Kids were trading one-liners, adults were catching up on the week, and it felt like six different conversations were happening simultaneously. I kept trying to ask the kids if they wanted water, sweet tea, or lemonade with their meal, but no one was listening to me. And instead of feeling frustrated, I felt so grateful. In fact, I turned to the sink, bowed my head, and prayed that I would hold the memory of those people and that night in my heart, that I would never forget the hundreds of ways I've experienced God's grace through those friends.

Then someone yelled for lemonade and the tender moment was over. But man, what treasure we have in one another. God is so good to give us life together.

Sometimes we get so used to people being around that we take them for granted. The sound of everyone talking and asking questions and occasionally even yelling gets to be a bit like white noise. So we don't typically stop in the middle of our day to appreciate how that one friend snorts a little bit when she laughs, or that other friend can't talk about dogs without crying, or another friend screams "DUDE!" when she is really enjoying something—whether it's some exceptional queso or the beachy wave effects of a new curling wand.

It seems like such simple, ordinary grace, but I'm not sure there's anything ordinary about living around and *enjoying* one another. Honestly, I think if we dig down into what it means to spend our lives in the company of other quirky, funny, unpredictable, interesting, occasionally awkward people—well, there's something spectacularly beautiful about it. There's genuine comfort there.

So when your sister interrupts you to remind you of when a boy made a heart with his hands like 2010-esque Justin Bieber? This is grace. Or when your mom throws her arms around you with such sincere affection that you're tempted to (lovingly) roll your eyes? This is grace. Or when a friend shouts a silly inside joke at you across campus? This is grace.

We are so incredibly fortunate to have one another, y'all. If you think about it, God didn't have to give us so much joy from our relationships. He could have created us, given us our earthly assignments, and let us live life without any real interaction with others. The fact that we get to take up residence in one another's hearts—that we get to learn from one another and love one another and miss one another—it's an undeserved gift of grace.

READ 1 THESSALONIANS 3:9–13.

1. As a general rule are you pretty grateful for the people around you? Or do they get on your nerves a little bit? (It's okay if they do.)

2. What are some quirky things your friends or family members do that bring you great joy? (For example, our friend Joey can make this super weird sound in his throat, and it never fails to make me laugh until I cry.)

3. What are a few of your favorite memories with other people? Were you grateful in the moment? Or were you more grateful when you looked back on those times?

4. Choose three times today when you're going to stop, look around— no matter where you are—and thank God for the people around you. If you need to set an alarm on your phone, do that.

TODAY'S PRAYER

Day 94

*W*hen I came to faith in Christ as a teenager, the music of Amy Grant was my soundtrack. Some of you have probably heard your moms talk about Amy Grant over the years, and that is because she was BELOVED among those of us who spent a good bit of time at church camps in the eighties and nineties.

I so associate Amy (we've never met, but I talk about her like she's a dear friend) with my early days of faith that I can't hear the song "All I Ever Have to Be" EVEN NOW without feeling all my "new creation in Christ" feelings. Amy was a voice of consistent encouragement, a reminder that while I might feel the conflict between old me and new me, I belonged to Jesus. Amy's music was a comfort when I wondered whether I truly had trusted in Jesus for my salvation. It brings back memories of standing up and declaring I wanted to follow Jesus at Camp Wesley Pines and of tearfully confessing to my youth group leader a few years later that I was struggling in my relationship with the Lord—and praying the prayer of salvation again.

Now, clearly, I've never had an actual conversation with Amy Grant about the arc and progression of my personal life with Jesus, but as I have listened to her music as an adult, I have realized there was something Amy understood about faith that flat-out eluded me when I was a teenager. I was so focused on my salvation experience—when it happened, how it happened, whether I was *really* assured that I would go to heaven—that I gave little thought to a reality that my friend Shaun expressed so succinctly several years ago: in addition to being saved *from* something, I had also been saved *for* something. I was so preoccupied with that first thing that I gave little consideration to the second. I had been saved *from* the consequences of my sin—no doubt about it—but I had not yet broken free of the self-absorption that kept me from seeing what I had been saved *for*.

My hope is that Amy would back me up when I say this: the moment you came to faith in Christ was a lavish gift of grace that forever shifted the eternal trajectory of your life. But it is ALSO an extravagantly gracious gift that as you live your life as a believer, you get to be part of seeking the Kingdom of God—the world as it should be and will be after Jesus' return—right where you are. (True story: right now there is a sticky note that says "SEEK THE KINGDOM" on my computer at work because I never want to forget my big-picture purpose.) I missed this part altogether when I was younger. When we belong to Jesus, the Holy Spirit is with us wherever we go. That means that in countless ways we get to seek His heart for the people around us in the communities where we live and work. We get to love the unloved, serve the lost, and help the poor. We get to act justly, seek mercy, and walk humbly (Micah 6:8). We get to join in God's work right here on earth, and as we do that, by God's grace, we offer the hurting world a glimpse of the Kingdom to come.

Thank God for saving grace that enables us to point people to the unconditional love and mercy of our heavenly Father. Thank God that we were saved to seek His Kingdom every day of our lives and reflect it here on earth.

READ 2 CORINTHIANS 5:16–21.

1. Do you remember when you came to faith in Christ? Write about that a little bit.

2. One time a family friend said she had trusted in Christ for salvation "about five times" (it's one of my favorite stories). Why do you think we can be so prone to question our salvation that we recommit our lives to Jesus over and over again?

3. Do you ever think about what you have been saved *for*? How do you feel compelled to love and serve in your community?

_____

_____

_____

4. Look up Matthew 6:33. Write/doodle/illustrate it here.

_____

_____

_____

TODAY'S PRAYER

_____

_____

_____

_____

_____

_____

_____

_____

_____

_____

_____

_____

Day 95

*J*t was still early in the morning when I saw her standing outside my door. I motioned for her to come into my office, and she had barely crossed the door's threshold when she spoke:

"Mrs. Sophie? Can you talk?"

I knew just by looking at her that whatever was on her mind was weighing heavy. I assured her I had nothing more important to do than listen to her, and we settled in on opposite ends of an L-shaped sectional sofa that has borne witness to more than its fair share of heartfelt conversations.

It's bad, she said, alternately fidgeting with her phone and wiping away her tears. For the next hour she told me about a series of events that had led to some significant regret and no small amount of shame. She teetered between crying and trying to be strong—not that those two things are mutually exclusive—and when she finished the first part of her story, I said these words: "Therefore, there is now no condemnation for those in Christ Jesus" (Romans 8:1). The girl who was sitting in my office all those years ago is someone who loves the Lord. She belongs to Him. She had confessed her sin to God and received His forgiveness. The situation she told me about would not and could not separate her from the love of Christ. This is essential to remember when we're embarrassed or ashamed about something we've done.

But as our conversation continued, I started to realize that while yes, she was deeply sorrowful about her actions that led up to our talk, she was even more brokenhearted by her continued struggle with the same areas of sin. *I feel like something is wrong with me*, she said. *I don't understand why I do better for a while, and then it gets bad again.*

This is the story for every single one of us, right? Sin can feel like such a vicious cycle because our desire to escape it can feel just as strong as our willingness to jump back in. I can think of two particular areas of sin in my own life where, on a Monday night, I would give you ten reasons why I was done with it forever, and then, on Tuesday, I could give you ten reasons why it wasn't that big of a problem after all. I once heard someone say that the enemy's strategy with sin is a brilliant one because he initially convinces you that it's no big deal, and then, after you're stuck in it, he convinces you that it's such a big deal that you'll never be able to recover from it. The girl in my office was living in that exact place.

So here's what I want to remind all of us: we do not fight sin alone. We have Jesus on our side. We have people who love us and pray for us. And I know—because I have seen it happen in my own life—the humbling, vulnerable process of confessing sin and receiving forgiveness is not in vain. There are things I struggled with twenty years ago that I don't even think about anymore. There are things I struggle with now that I pray will lose their grip on me in the future. We cannot overcome any of this in our own strength, but as we know and love Jesus more, we will, by His grace, see how His love can repair what sin has broken. And that love will overshadow temptation. That love will pave the way to healing. What grace!

READ PSALM 51:10–13.

1. Have you ever felt like the girl in my office—utterly frustrated by repeated sin in your life? Write about that a little.

2. Do you feel like you have two or three areas of sin that can keep you caught in a vicious cycle? What are they?

3. Do you feel like you can talk honestly to the Lord about these struggles? What's the part of that sin that draws you in? What's the part that makes you want to be done forever?

4. Do you ever feel embarrassed or ashamed because of these struggles? Who do you talk to about that?

TODAY'S PRAYER

Day 96

*A*s hard as it is for me to believe, we've hit the stage of family life where we're starting to talk about college a lot in our house. We have a few college visits scheduled this spring, and I'm anxious to see the dorms so that I can get a good idea about where I'll be living.

OH, I AM TOTALLY KIDDING.

There are apparently eleventy hundred components to this whole college selection and admission process, and one of the most important happened yesterday: Alex took the ACT. He took it at school last winter, but this was the first time he has taken it as a junior. And like every stereotypical parent, I couldn't wait to hear what he thought.

He started by telling me about the English portion, knowing I was especially interested in the subject (English teacher habits die hard, y'all). Then he mentioned that he had to take a second math test—which I had never, ever heard of—and said that it was the hardest section of all. I asked him what made it so difficult, and he said, *I had never seen that kind of math. I didn't even know what the problems were asking me to do. Some of those math problems had exclamation points!*

For an English major like me, this boggles the mind. Fortunately, we found out today that his second math test won't factor into his score; it was just ACT's way of testing some new problems. Even still, I totally empathized with my son, who had to sit in front of those problems for thirty minutes with little idea how to solve them. As someone who may have been kicked all the way out of honors math in high school, I can easily relate to mathematical confusion.

I've been thinking about that second math test off and on this afternoon, and it has reminded me that we will inevitably face situations or circumstances in our lives that will puzzle us—where we'll have no idea what to do. It may be that a family conflict gets complicated, or a job offer requires moving to a different state, or someone we thought we could trust turns out to be not-so-trustworthy.

There are lots of ways you can approach perplexing situations. You can pray. You can look to Scripture. These are both great ideas. But just like I would have sent Alex straight to a qualified tutor if he was going to have to tackle the unfamiliar math again, we can adopt a similar spiritual strategy when it's hard to find our way forward. The wisdom, perspective, and insight of a trusted family member, pastor, mentor, or counselor is invaluable. I'm not saying it's not great to step out in personal faith—because sometimes that's what the Lord asks us to do—but when we're in situations where seeking wise counsel from someone who loves the Lord (and has walked with Him awhile!) is an option, we need to run with that. The other person can't make your decision, of course, but they can help you think through the best next steps, and they can point you in the direction of peace when it's hard to know which way to turn.

Thank the Lord for wise mentors today. They are His grace in action when we face tough decisions.

READ 1 JOHN 4:1–4.

1. When was the last time you felt totally, genuinely confused? Was it something as straightforward as learning a challenging concept in chemistry? Was it something relational? Something concerning your future?

_____

_____

_____

2. Do you have a preferred way to work through confusing problems? Do you like to make a list of pros and cons? Go for a run? Sleep on it?

_____

_____

_____

3. Who are some of the trusted older voices in your life?

4. Is there any situation that's confounding you right now? Explain.

TODAY'S PRAYER

Day 97

*T*he girls I work with at my school love being in a stage of life where there are an endless number of possibilities ahead. However, those very endless possibilities can also be overwhelming. Senior girls often experience an underlying feeling of HOW DO I KNOW WHAT TO DO? their last year in high school, and the part of my personality that likes to help people solve problems is always tempted to jump in and offer suggestions. LET ME MAKE IT BETTER!

A couple of years ago, though, I had an experience that made me rethink our culture's collective tendency to anticipate every possible option for the future. Don't get me wrong. I am always happy to have a discussion with someone who is trying to sort out what's ahead, but sometimes I think we create unnecessary anxiety with our hyperfocus on those decisions.

So. One winter weekend I drove to Nashville to speak at a church retreat for junior high and high school girls. When I arrived, I called the girls' minister, Amy Jo, to see where I would be staying. There were cabins all over the place, and I wanted to unload all of my stuff before heading to that night's session.

Amy Jo's response surprised me: *Well, we wanted you to have a place that was private, so you'll be staying in the infirmary.* It wasn't the news I was expecting, but I followed Amy Jo's directions, found the infirmary, and put my luggage and linens in a nurse's room right off the lobby area. Since I could tell the building was large, I did some exploring before heading back to the main meeting area. There were two large treatment rooms with about ten beds each, then another, smaller treatment room with probably five beds. So I was the only person staying in a building that could sleep roughly *twenty-five* people.

I'm not gonna lie. It was one of the most surreal lodging experiences of my life. Later that night, when I was trying to fall asleep in the screaming quiet of that big, empty building, I thought, *Lord, I could never have expected this. Not in a million years. How could I have even anticipated it? I AM ABOUT TO SLEEP IN AN EMPTY INFIRMARY.* And then the Lord and I had a good chuckle about it all. (Pretty sure the Lord thinks my reactions are hilarious.)

That particular weekend—with that particular group of girls—turned out to be one of my favorites. When I left that campground at the end of the retreat, I was overwhelmed by God's grace. The weekend was nothing I expected (after all, I slept in an empty infirmary) and everything I needed. It was a reminder that Jesus doesn't just give us life; He gives us the unexpected. He gives us adventure! He gives us exceedingly and abundantly more than we can ask or imagine (Ephesians 3:20).

That's why, when girls come by my office and feel completely overwhelmed by future possibilities, I am delighted to remind them that when they love Jesus and commit their lives to Him, they might not end up where they expect, but they won't miss a thing. Because even when we're not sure where we're going—and have no idea what might be next— walking through the doors Jesus opens will be the biggest adventure, and the biggest blast, we will ever have.

READ PSALM 84:9–12.

1. Do you find some comfort in making detailed plans? Or do you prefer to roll with it and see what happens? Explain that a little bit.

2. How far down the road have you gotten with your planning? Let me put it this way: Have you thought about cities where you might love to live? Your perfect career? Possible names for future kids?

3. When you think about the phrase "follow Jesus," what does that mean to you?

_____

_____

_____

4. Do you think about your life with God as an adventure with unexpected twists and turns? Is that something that you want? Why or why not?

_____

_____

_____

TODAY'S PRAYER

_____

_____

_____

_____

_____

_____

_____

_____

Day 98

*S*everal summers ago, when Alex and I traveled to Kenya, we flew on a tiny airplane to the Maasai Mara National Reserve on the next-to-last day of our trip. We landed on a dirt airstrip, jumped on a two-hour safari ride, and then checked in at the place we were staying. It was actually an open-air lodge (hot tip: whenever someone uses the phrase "open air," that's code for "air conditioning is unavailable"), and our rooms were understated but stunning tent structures. There was a wood floor and a bathroom in each tent, but the vaulted ceiling, back wall, and windows were canvas.

After a second (stunning!) safari ride at dusk, we headed back to the lodge after sunset. Our group—nine of us, I think—went to dinner in the lodge's dining room, and I had just started to eat my potato and leek soup when one of the lodge's managers approached our table.

"I'm so sorry to interrupt," he said softly, in the loveliest, lilting Kenyan accent, "but which of you is staying in number 27?" It took a few seconds before I realized that Alex and I were in 27. And while the manager's accent made me want to believe I had been chosen for a dance contest or some such revelry, I anticipated that the news probably wasn't good. After the manager asked me a few questions about what items I might have left in the tent, I asked if everything was okay. I was not at all prepared for his answer.

"Well, ma'am," he replied very calmly, "it would seem, you see, that the, um, *monkeys* have gotten into your tent."

"What?" I asked, likely way too loudly. "THE MONKEYS?" And then: "Sir, if you don't mind me asking, how in the world did the monkeys get in our tent?"

"Oh," he said excitedly, "the monkeys are very clever!"

As it turned out, the monkeys had opened an unsecured zipper on one of the tent's canvas windows—apparently unable to resist the lure of a bag of pistachio nuts I had left on the desk. While everything was ultimately fine, the monkeys did have some fun with our suitcases. As one of the stewards mentioned the next morning, "Clothes were strewn everywhere!"

And that, my friends, is a perfect metaphor for how life feels sometimes: like monkeys have gotten all up in our business. We realize that we're walking through about fourteen high-stress situations at the same time, and it's hard to see the Lord at work because we're so preoccupied by difficult circumstances. It might be that we invited the disruptiveness with our choices (hey there, pistachio nuts), or it might just be that our jam-packed calendar has left us with very little margin. But when life feels crazy, remember this:

1. **Stay calm (2 Timothy 1:7).** Screaming at the monkeys won't make them go away. Neither will taking out your frustrations on the people who love you most. Give yourself room to process and pray.

2. **Hold on (Psalm 63:8).** Jesus never changes, never waivers, and never bolts. He is not put off by your heartache, your crisis, or your schedule. Cling to Him when you're overwhelmed.

3. **Give thanks (Psalm 28:7).** There are good lessons even in the hard moments. Even when life feels chaotic, the Lord is at work. Give Him glory.

Remember, the monkeys won't stick around forever. This, too, is grace!

READ 1 CORINTHIANS 16:13–14.

1. How do you typically handle disruptions in your life? Do you become stone-cold calm? Or do you tend to freak out a little? Explain.

2. What "monkeys" are currently all up in your business? What feels disruptive in your life right now?

3. Are you doing anything to lure in the hypothetical monkeys? Are you overcommitting? Saying yes to too much? Trying to keep too many people happy? Working so hard to build your resume that your stress level is off the charts? Write about your answer a little bit.

4. Look up 2 Corinthians 4:8. Write/doodle/illustrate it here.

TODAY'S PRAYER

Day 99

*A*s we get close to the end of the book, I want to tell you one of my absolute FAVORITE stories from the Bible. It was early on a Sunday morning—still dark outside—and I imagine that Mary Magdalene's heart was practically beating outside her chest as she approached the tomb. Jesus had been crucified two days before, and she expected His body would still be there. To Mary Magdalene's utter surprise, though, the stone that sealed off the tomb had been rolled away, and Jesus' body was nowhere to be found. Her first thought? *Somebody moved Him.*

Mary Magdalene ran to the disciples, and Peter and John followed her back to the tomb. Peter saw that the linens that covered Jesus were still there—along with the cloth that had been wrapped around His head—and when John saw the same, Scripture tells us that he "saw and believed" (John 20:8). The two men returned to the other disciples (perhaps to tell them a miracle had happened) while Mary Magdalene remained at the tomb. She longed to see Jesus' body. She wept.

Mary Magdalene looked inside the tomb again—even telling the angels that someone had taken her Lord away—and when she turned around, Jesus was standing in front of her, only she didn't realize it was Him. And when He asked why she was crying, she gave Him the same answer she had given the angels: someone had taken her Lord away.

Then—this part brings me to tears every single time—Jesus said her name: "Mary" (v. 16). She responded in Hebrew by exclaiming "Teacher!" And He told her to "go to my brothers and tell them that I am ascending to my Father and your Father, to my God and your God" (v. 17).

Just typing out this story makes me a weepy mess. But I want to be sure to point out five ways Mary Magdalene's (MM's) relationship with Jesus can encourage us:

1. **MM followed Jesus.** Before Mary Magdalene ever showed up at the tomb, Jesus had healed her (Luke 8:2); she had followed Him and learned from Him. She had also witnessed His crucifixion

(John 19:25–26) and burial (Mark 15:47). After Jesus healed her, she devoted her life to Him. We want to be women who do the same.

2. **MM loved Jesus.** After the heartbreak of seeing Jesus crucified, she showed up at His tomb before dawn. When she realized the tomb was empty, she was desperate to find Him. In her uncertainty and her grief, she cried. Unlike MM, we don't have to wonder where Jesus' physical body is, but like her, we should seek to know Him and love Him with our whole hearts (Acts 17:27).

3. **MM was known by Jesus.** Jesus called her by name, just as He does us (Isaiah 43:1).

4. **MM believed Jesus.** When Jesus told Mary that He would be ascending "to my Father and your Father," she didn't question Him. We should also take Jesus at His word. What He says is true (Matthew 22:16).

5. **MM was the first person to proclaim the resurrection of Jesus.** Don't miss this. A woman was the first person to proclaim the Good News of Jesus' resurrection. You do the same, my sister. Do not hesitate to share what the Lord has done and is doing in your life (Psalm 71:17); use your voice and the gifts He has given you to make His name known!

The grace of God enables you to follow Jesus, love Jesus, believe Jesus, know Jesus, and proclaim the Good News of Jesus. Live boldly today in His name!

READ 1 CORINTHIANS 16:13–14.

1. What improbable things had to have occurred for Mary Magdalene to discover the stone had been rolled away and the tomb was empty?

2. Have you ever experienced desperation when you discovered something was not as you expected? Or when you felt like you'd lost something (whether that was a physical object or something intangible, like trust)?

3. Look at the five ways we can be encouraged by Mary Magdalene's relationship with Jesus. Which one touches you the most? Why?

4. Which of those five truths do you most want to carry into your day today? Why?

TODAY'S PRAYER

Day 100

*W*ell, here we are. After one hundred days—which, I have to say, was quite a commitment on your part—you've made it to the last day of this book. I am so proud of you! As we wrap up, there are a couple of things I want to be sure to tell you: (1) Thank you for your patience with all the devotions about my walks at the park. I know there were about seven (or fifty) of them. For a while there, the pandemic really limited my life outside my house. I feel like you understand. And (2) I'm really going to miss you. I know that might sound weird because, well, *we've probably never met*, but one of the sweet things the Lord has done during this book-writing process is to have given me deep, almost inexplicable affection for the people who will read these devotions. I am humbled and honored that you have joined me on these pages. You are God's grace to me!

So. Now that we're on the one hundredth day, we've clearly spent a lot of time together, and I pray that as you close this book for the final time, you're more confident in—and aware of—the grace of God than you were on Day One. I pray that on days when you feel discouraged or disappointed or disillusioned, you'll remember that while there are many things God can do, there are two things He cannot: He cannot lie, and He cannot fail. Trust Him with every part of your life. He is faithful.

In the first devotional book I wrote, I closed it with a commissioning, and I want to do that again. Because even though I don't know the specifics of what your life will look like in the days and months and years to come, I do know this: The Lord has good plans for you (Jeremiah 29:11). The Lord will make a way for you (Isaiah 43:19). And because you belong to Him, His grace covers you (James 4:6).

By the way, this is one of those times where I wish you could play an audio clip as you read because I would love to speak this commissioning over you. Since you can't hear me, though, just add a strong Southern accent when you read this in your head.

My sister in Christ,
You are a beloved child of the Creator of the universe.
Your life is a gift from God.
Your life is a gift to the world.
And because you belong to Jesus, your life bears witness—your life testifies—to the unmerited, undeserved, relentless grace of God.
So, daughter of the King, remember:
God's grace is at work in you.
When you feel conviction, turn from sin, walk in repentance, love your neighbor, receive forgiveness, seek the Kingdom, and chase after the heart of your heavenly Father—all of this is grace.
God's grace is all around you.
When you watch the sunset, smell fresh honeysuckle, hear a baby's laugh, feel invigorated by a workout, catch a glimpse of fresh green leaves against a crystal blue sky, or share a smile with a friend who knows what you're thinking when you haven't said a word—all of this is grace.
God's grace is with you wherever you go.
When you help a stranger, care for the hurting, show mercy, pursue justice, extend forgiveness, share the Gospel, or give without expecting anything in return— all of this is grace.
And finally, always remember: you can never outrun the grace of God.
It covers you completely.
Rest in it. Believe it.
And, every chance you have, share it.
In Jesus' name. Amen.

READ PSALM 90:14–17.

1. What are three things you think you'll remember from the last one hundred days?

2. What feels like the grace of God in your life right now? List those things—and thank the Lord for them.

3. Is there a particular area of your life where you're experiencing renewed hope, fresh encouragement, or maybe even an unexpected sense of peace? Write about that a little bit.

4. Read John 1:16. Write/doodle/illustrate it here.

TODAY'S PRAYER